PRAISE FOR
PUBLISH WITH PURPOSE

This book is absolutely packed with the most meaningful and valuable insights into publishing your book for today's author. A "must have" for any author pursuing tremendous success while following a tried and true publishing strategy. Don't write another word without first devouring *Publish With Purpose*. LOVE IT!

Annie Jennings
acclaimed publicity expert and
CEO of the famous national PR firm, Annie Jennings PR

I love the whole concept behind *Publish with Purpose* because I believe in the power of books to make a difference in the world. This brief guide covers many important topics you need to consider when writing a book with a mission. Highly recommended!

Stephanie Chandler
author of *The Nonfiction Book Publishing Plan* and
CEO of the Nonfiction Authors Association

Tara Alemany packs a lot of wisdom and dead-on advice in this guide to knowing what you want to accomplish and who you want to serve with your next book. I highly recommend it.

Sandra Beckwith
author and book marketing coach, Build Book Buzz

Tara Alemany and her new book *Publish with Purpose* are a remarkable resource for all authors. The book not only helps authors plot their course, but create an impactful and meaningful manuscript and bring it to life. Writing isn't easy, but this book helps readers make thoughtful and strategic decisions to build their brand, connect with their audience, and create a strong branding opportunity in the form of a polished and well-written book. No matter where you end your journey as an author, this is where you should begin.

Justin Spizman
Book Architect and Georgia Author of the Year

Tara Alemany has made a name for herself as a recognized leader in the publishing industry. I wish I had this book when I was trying to navigate my journey to market.

Angelina Assanti
President of the Florida Authors and Publishers Association

Tara published this book with a purpose. That purpose being to help you get the book you've always wanted to write out of your head and into the hands of eager readers, where it can do your career the most good. Her "no fluff" writing style gets right to the point. You'll discover the many benefits of being a published author that you may not have considered before, and see case studies where her clients are using what she shares in this book to great success. Her deep knowledge and experience in the publishing industry is evident and you'll learn how to connect with your reader even before you write a single word to achieve the success you want most!

Robert Imbriale
business coach and host of Coach's Corner Podcast

Want a simple way to share the vision and goals for your book with your editor, book designer, marketing team and publicist? The exercises in *Publish with Purpose* will give you the tools you need, and your team will thank you for it!

Michele DeFilippo
owner, 1106 Design

PUBLISH WITH PURPOSE

PUBLISH
WITH
PURPOSE

A Goal-Oriented Framework
for Publishing Success

TARA R. ALEMANY
Foreword by Penny Sansevieri

EMERALD LAKE
BOOKS

Publish with Purpose: A Goal-Oriented Framework for Publishing Success

Copyright © 2019 Tara R. Alemany

Cover design by Mark Gerber

Cover illustration copyright © 2019 Mark Gerber

Some of the links included in this book may be affiliate links. This means if you purchase an item through an affiliate link, Emerald Lake Books will receive a commission. We only recommend products and services we believe in. However, you should always evaluate a product or service yourself before making a buying decision from anyone.

Books published by Emerald Lake Books may be ordered through your favorite booksellers or by visiting emeraldlakebooks.com.

ISBN: 978-1-945847-15-8 (paperback)
       978-1-945847-16-5 (epub)
       978-1-945847-18-9 (large print)
       978-1-945847-19-6 (audiobook)

Library of Congress Control Number: 2019904145

*This book is dedicated
to our Emerald Lake Books authors,
past, present and future.*

Thank you for allowing us
to dream with you
and, in so doing,
discover the things we need to know
to be the best we can be.

CONTENTS

FOREWORD

IN MY 19 YEARS in the book marketing business, I've discovered that the one thing, and main thing, that authors forget to consider is goals. When I speak to authors and ask them what their goals are, they always say, "book sales." But this isn't a goal—this is a by-product of having good goals and following the reader path.

When Tara first asked if I'd write the foreword for this book, I was honored, but also wasn't sure what to expect. Frankly, there are a lot of books on the market about publishing. But as I turned the pages of this book, I was pleased to discover that *Publish with Purpose* is unlike any other you've read before.

Yes, it's a book on writing. Sort of... And it's also a book on marketing. Sort of... But what it really is, is a cross-over book that looks at how writing and marketing (and everything else you do related to your book) are interconnected.

And that's what makes this book different.

Identifying your goals early on will help you in ways I can't even properly articulate. Many times, I see authors jump into the deep end of the swimming pool that is "publishing." They paddle around, hoping for the best. And while the idea of jumping in is certainly admirable, this will rarely lead to a successful pursuit of your dreams.

Authors often (okay, always) ask me what sells books, and the truth is... no one knows for sure. But most of us who have been in the industry know what does not sell books, and launching your publishing journey without large and small goals never leads to success.

They say that "success leaves clues" and this is incredibly true. When you look at successful authors who are doing well, and selling books, there is one constant with them—they have a plan and a strategy, and they keep after it, over and over again. And that's where this book comes in.

The exercises and case studies Tara has brilliantly crafted in this book will help you set your own goals. And, as we already know, real goals, especially goals that focus on reader engagement, aren't only more lucrative, they're more rewarding psychologically, and they'll push you to keep going even when things get hard.

So, I encourage you to read this book, do the exercises, and identify the goals that mean the most to you to pursue. Because these goals will help identify the most productive marketing tactics for you and your book, and that will take some of the "chore" out of being a successful writer.

Plus, charting your success against the goals you create, instead of purely sales, will make for a much more satisfying journey, even as your book sales naturally increase.

Penny Sansevieri
CEO, Author Marketing Experts

Introduction

I GREW UP *LOVING* BOOKS. They were my escape—my safe haven in a home filled with great turmoil. They were also my classroom and playground. They made me braver than I believed, stronger than I feared, and smarter than I thought.

As an adult, books have exposed me to more mentors than I could ever work with directly, allowing me to grow into the entrepreneur and human being I want to be. Any knowledge I could ever want is forever at my fingertips thanks to books. I can learn from experts who are popular today or sages who lived hundreds of years ago. And through books I have written, I can speak to thought leaders who are yet to come.

It was only when I began to sit on the other side of the page, as the one to write the words for someone else to learn from and escape into, that I finally saw that being an author was so much more than just imparting knowledge. It was granting freedom, both to my reader as well as myself.

When I wrote books for my business, it spared me from having to work in close contact with people who didn't appreciate what I had to offer. By letting people experience my unique brand of expertise and humor, they could decide whether I was a good fit for them without any pressure from me or my having to endure the agony of cold calling prospects.

Writing my books opened doors to speaking engagements, joint ventures, partner collaborations and other opportunities that grew my business organically. And this enabled me to attract clients who were a good fit to work with my company rather than going through the awkward cycle of pitching my services and hoping for a positive response.

I learned along the way that there is a right way and a wrong way to do this. Let me start first with the wrong way, because this book is all about how to do it the right way. And the wrong way is something I see happen way too often.

The wrong way to write a book is to sit down and do a brain dump of everything you want to say.

What? Isn't that what we're supposed to do? Share all our deep wisdom and knowledge?

The answer is "yes," but it must be done within a certain framework.

Let me share a quick story to illustrate my point.

When I was in my 20s and 30s, I spent years working in computer software development. I was a technical writer, and I often served as the liaison between software developers and the end-users who would be working with the software when it was released.

The developers were happy little coders who created functionality they thought would be useful, cool or just plain fun to use. But oftentimes, they did their development work with little input from the users. And we regularly discovered that the techies had no idea how real people were going to be using their software. So the functionality or interfaces the developers thought would be good to create repeatedly caused problems for those required to use the system.

I often see the same thing happen when people write a book (or even content for their website).

These authors are guilty of writing the content they want to share with little thought regarding who they're writing it for. They have a message they're passionate about sharing, so the exercise is more about getting out the words that are in their heads than communicating with someone specific.

While that technique may work well for some fiction writers, it defeats the purpose of writing a book for most nonfiction authors—and, indeed, quite a few fiction writers as well.

Most nonfiction writers have a specific message they want to communicate, and if they do that without giving thought to who their audience is, their message can easily fall flat.

And fiction writers targeting, for instance, a juvenile market need to spend quite a bit of time considering their reader. They need to align the vocabulary they use and the information they share with the grade levels of the kids who will be reading their books, especially if they hope to get their texts and stories into school systems.

Goal-Oriented Publishing

Seeing how frequently books are written without regard to their readers led us to develop a process that we use with the authors we work with at our publishing company, Emerald Lake Books. We call this technique our "goal-oriented publishing" framework.

This framework consists of three main parts, each of which aligns with a certain set of activities and stage of the publishing process.

✓ The first focuses on the reader and the experience the author wants them to have.

✓ The second addresses the author and their business, even if their business is only as a professional writer.

✓ And the third area concentrates on the book and its overall impact.

Each focus involves different activities and yields different benefits, and we'll go through those in more detail in the pages that follow.

But by creating goals for each of these focus areas, this framework enables the author to be more intentional about their writing, the design of the book, their marketing plan, and the supporting materials needed for their book. It also redefines what "success" means to them. Instead of focusing on selling a specific number of books as their benchmark for success, the author shifts their focus to the outcomes they want their reader to experience, their business to achieve, and their book to create.

The sad truth is, most books never sell more than 250 copies over their lifetimes. But we consistently find that, when our process is used, our authors easily sell those 250 copies or more during the first few months after their launch. Much of their success comes down to the fact that they're not focusing on book sales but on other measures they feel passionate about and capable of achieving. The sales just naturally follow.

The aim of goal-oriented publishing is to help you see beyond your book to the impact you can have when you publish with a specific purpose in mind.

KNOW YOUR IDEAL CUSTOMER

BEFORE WE DIVE into the goal-oriented publishing framework, though, let's take a moment to define the ideal customer for your business.

For those of you who are writing because you're a professional author, this customer is the person who will purchase your book, but not necessarily the one who will read it. For example, in the case of children's books, it is rare for kids to actually be the buyers. Usually it's a parent, grandparent, librarian or teacher who purchases the book for them to enjoy.

However, if you're writing this book to build another business, this is the client you hope to attract after they have read your book.

Create a Customer Avatar

If you've ever worked with a business coach or a customer relationship management system (CRM), one of the first things they probably had you do was create a customer or client avatar. This is a fictional character that represents a composite of your ideal customer or client. When it's complete, you'll have a better understanding of the underlying motivating beliefs, fears and secret desires that influence their buying decisions.

Google the term "client avatar template" or "customer avatar template" and you'll find a variety of resources to help you. Hubspot (elbks.com/hubspot) and DigitalMarketer (elbks.com/digitalmarketer) both provide templates we think work well.

To give you an idea of what goes into a customer avatar, we'll share two of ours. They follow a simple format derived from the Hubspot and DigitalMarketer templates, where we describe the following:

- ✓ **Basic demographics** – Understand who they are as a person and what their life circumstances are like. This can help strengthen the bond between you and define targeting options in advertising. It can also be a guide as you brainstorm service and product offerings that fit their unique circumstances.

- ✓ **Goals/Aspirations** – Be clear on their goals and aspirations, so you know what they're trying to accomplish. This may serve to drive the products and services you offer as you grow, as well as help you write copy that resonates with this audience.

- ✓ **Values** – Discover what they're committed to being and doing, and how they want to show up in the world. As with understanding their goals and aspirations, understanding what they value ensures you can communicate with them in language that captures their hearts and minds.

- ✓ **Information sources** – Identify their favorite sources of information. This may suggest potential advertising and targeting options when it comes time to connect with them.

- ✓ **Challenges** – Explore the difficulties your ideal client is facing. When you can demonstrate that you provide solutions to those problems, you'll have their full attention.

✓ **Pain points** – Go beyond just the challenges they face to look more closely at what causes them pain. Oftentimes, this is associated with a failure or a fear they have, and it will fuel many of their objections to working with you. Demonstrating sensitivity to that pain point while showing how your solution addresses them will be key to gaining their trust.

✓ **Objections to the sale** – Identify any objections they may have to the sale so that you can address them before they arise, as often as possible.

You are welcome to create as many client avatars as you need to define your customer base. However, if your marketing is to be effective, it's not reasonable to market to more than one avatar at a time.

The best way to formulate your client avatar is to look at your existing customer base and see what commonalities you can find in the clients you enjoy working with the most. Then, create a list of the thoughts, experiences and characteristics they share in common. Evaluate it to see if there are other traits you'd like your ideal customer to have or variations on existing traits that work equally well for you. Then, consider whether there are traits in the list that don't work well for building the business you want, and remove all of those.

While this exercise is always easier to do once you have a history of sales, social media engagement and website traffic to look back on, that doesn't mean you can't complete it if you are new in business. If you don't have existing customers to base it on, imagine who you'd like to have buy your books, products or services (whatever it is you sell). Do you have a friend or neighbor who would be an ideal customer for you?

Use them to formulate your list of thoughts, experiences and characteristics.

The important thing to remember is, if you're following our methodology, you aren't creating your avatar right now. While most client avatar templates will have you jump right into creating your avatar, the way we do it is a bit different.

We have you start by listing the important elements that define the viewpoint, background and behaviors of your ideal customer. It's only after we've created these lists that we're going to mix and match elements to create specific avatars for marketing purposes. Approaching your avatar this way enables you to quickly and easily create numerous avatars without a significant amount of extra effort.

The Brainstormed List

For your brainstormed list, focus on each specific area of the avatar you'll eventually want to create.

- ✓ Basic information
- ✓ Goals and aspirations
- ✓ Values
- ✓ Information sources
- ✓ Challenges
- ✓ Pain points
- ✓ Objections to the sale

When you begin listing **basic information** about the person, this doesn't necessarily include typical demographic information (like gender, age, education and marital status). For this part of the exercise, those may not be necessary to paint a clear picture of your ideal client and where they are in life. But you'll want to add them later, when you create your avatar.

To give an example, we describe our ideal customers as "positive people who have an engaging, exciting or entertaining message to share with the world." While we often will work with an author who is a successful entrepreneur hoping to use their book to deliver an important message and help grow their business, that's not always the case.

For their basic information, our ideal customer has at least 5 of the following characteristics:

- ✓ In business a minimum of 3 years.
- ✓ In business 5-7 years.
- ✓ In business 8-10 years.
- ✓ In business 10+ years.
- ✓ Annual business revenue of at least $125K.
- ✓ Annual business revenue of at least $250K.
- ✓ Annual business revenue of at least $500K.
- ✓ Annual business revenue of $1M+.
- ✓ Develops new products or services to keep clients coming back.
- ✓ Develops new message to keep clients coming back.
- ✓ Has multiple levels of services.
- ✓ Plans to have multiple levels of services.
- ✓ Has worked with a business coach, so they understand the value of receiving guidance from an expert.
- ✓ Attends business conferences, TEDx talks or industry conferences to network and gain more visibility.

- ✓ Speaks at business conferences, TEDx talks or industry conferences to network and gain more visibility.
- ✓ Participates in an organization that freely supports, connects and promotes its members.
- ✓ Participates in an organization where members freely support, connect and promote each other.
- ✓ The manuscript is ready (or almost ready) to edit or to be submitted to a publisher.
- ✓ Is within 30-45 days of making a decision about which publisher to work with.
- ✓ Is based in the U.S.

You may note that some of the characteristics seem contradictory, like "Has multiple levels of services" and "Plans to have multiple levels of services." But that's because we'll pick one or the other for our avatar. Both work well for our business, so either one is acceptable to us.

However, the more of these traits a potential customer has, the better a match they are for our business.

Here's a list of the **goals and aspirations** of our ideal customer:

- ✓ Has a story, but needs to clarify the message.
- ✓ Knows their audience.
- ✓ Is passionate about their topic and convinced that it's worthwhile and will help others.
- ✓ Loves to dig deeper into their area of expertise.
- ✓ Is intellectually curious and values learning.
- ✓ Enjoys the writing process and is committed to sharing what they know.

✓ Has a business that is running well, but wants to become a recognized leader.

✓ Is a recognized leader whose business is running well, but wants this book to enter a new space or refresh an existing message.

✓ Recognizes the need to keep their message fresh, so will publish every 2–3 years.

✓ Sees that growth is leveling off and recognizes the need to invest for new growth.

✓ Values building their sphere of influence through networking and social media.

✓ Recognizes that a book is a means to achieve a higher quality of life for themselves and their family.

✓ Has calculated business growth goals rather than being driven by "New Year's resolutions."

✓ Has an achievable goal for business and sees a book as laying the groundwork for success.

✓ Doesn't know much about publishing, and wants help to do that.

✓ Recognizes the benefits of having the right people doing the right jobs.

✓ Values professionalism.

✓ Wants to capitalize on the expertise of others.

✓ Is interested in and actively pursuing personal development opportunities.

✓ Wants to grow as a person.

✓ Seeks to break through to the next level and is intent on getting it right.

✓ Is willing to look for guidance to shortcut the process.

✓ Likes to recommend good resources to people they care about and connects people to each other in their network.

✓ Is excited about writing a book and wants to learn more about the publishing process.

✓ Is excited about writing a book, but doesn't want to participate any more than necessary in the publishing process.

Once again, you'll see some conflicting elements, but that's because we're going to mix and match these variations to create a specific avatar that will represent the person we're trying to reach with a specific campaign.

They get most of their business **information** from these sources:

✓ Reads *Inc.*

✓ Reads *Forbes.*

✓ Reads *Business Insider.*

✓ Reads *HuffPost.*

✓ Reads Hearst Media (regional media).

✓ Reads trade journals and industry news sites.

✓ Follows Brendon Burchard.

✓ Follows Darren Hardy.

✓ Follows Mike Michalowicz.

✓ Follows Tony Robbins.

✓ Follows Russell Brunson.

✓ Watches TEDx Talks.

✓ Watches Shark Tank.

✓ Attends at least one webinar a month.

These are some of the **challenges** our ideal customer faces:

✓ Realizes that visibility is not yet as broad as needed to achieve business goals.

✓ Understands the importance of having a social platform, but is not using it as efficiently as they can.

✓ Has at least 1,000 followers across all platforms, but recognizes the need for a larger following.

✓ Wants to 10x their following.

The **pain points** they're wrestling with include the following:

✓ Tried to write a book on their own in the past, and it hasn't worked out for them.

✓ Tried to publish a book on their own in the past, and it hasn't worked out for them.

✓ Tried to build their business with a book on their own in the past, and it hasn't worked out for them.

✓ Knows there are better uses of their gifts and talents than continuing to try to figure it out on their own.

✓ Is so passionate about this book that it's almost driving them mad that they can't get it done faster. The book is driving them forward, rather than them trying to push it out. It's taken on a life of its own, and they need someone to help them with the birthing process.

And their **objections** to buying our services include the following:

- ✓ Is concerned about the exclusive license clause in our publishing agreement.
- ✓ Worries about the cost of our services: will they sell enough copies to cover the cost of publishing?
- ✓ Don't want to change what they've written.

Once you've created your own lists for each of these sections, it's easy to mix and match qualities to create as many different avatars as you want. And because they are each based on qualities you know are important to you, they will all work. It's just a matter of fine-tuning the messaging so that it resonates with the right people.

The more details you can provide that illustrate the complexities of your ideal customer, the better you'll be able to target your content and marketing.

Creating Your Avatar

For many of the customer avatar templates you'll find on the internet, this is where they have you jump in. We find it a bit more challenging to start here, though, because there are so many qualities that are shared among our ideal customers. The avatars are more often about the differences between them. So, when we have a list of everything that's true about our ideal customers, it almost doesn't matter how they are combined to create an avatar, which makes this part of the process so much easier. After all, when it's hard to go wrong, why wrestle with it so much?

Oftentimes, this is where adding more demographic information helps, even if those demographics don't matter as much to your business. For example, we work with both male and female authors, so gender is not a defining characteristic for our ideal list of traits. But when marketing to someone, we can help readers self-select more easily if we're specific about who we're talking to.

So, pulling from our lists that I shared earlier, here are two distinct avatars that would both work well for us. We've added in some personal demographic information by using the insights from our social profiles and analytics from our website to see who's already interested in what we have to offer. This enables us to refine our marketing copy and advertising targeting to reach our ideal customers more effectively.

MEET VERONICA WORDSMITH

Basic Demographics:

- ✓ Female, aged 45–65 years.
- ✓ Lives within a 75-mile radius of New York City.
- ✓ In business 7 years.
- ✓ Annual business revenue of $135,000.
- ✓ Plans to have multiple levels of services.
- ✓ Has worked with a business coach, so she understands the value of receiving expert guidance.
- ✓ Participates in an organization that freely supports, connects and promotes each other.
- ✓ Has a manuscript ready to edit and is ready to begin working with a publisher.

Goals/Aspirations:

- ✓ Has a story, but needs to clarify the message.
- ✓ Is passionate about her topic and convinced that it's worthwhile and will help others.

- ✓ Loves to dig deeper into her area of expertise.
- ✓ Has a business that is running well, but wants to become a recognized leader.
- ✓ Has an achievable goal for business and sees a book as laying the groundwork for success.
- ✓ Doesn't know much about publishing, but wants help to do that.
- ✓ Is willing to look for guidance to shortcut the process.

Information Sources:

- ✓ Reads *Forbes*.
- ✓ Reads *HuffPost*.
- ✓ Follows Brendon Burchard.
- ✓ Follows Darren Hardy.
- ✓ Watches TEDx Talks.
- ✓ Attends at least one webinar a month.

Challenges:

- ✓ Knows visibility is not yet as broad as it needs to be to achieve business goals.
- ✓ Wants to 10x her following.

Pain Points:

- ✓ Tried to build her business with a book on her own in the past, and it hasn't worked out for her.
- ✓ This book has taken on a life of its own, and she needs help with the birthing process.

Objection to Sale:

✓ The cost of our services: will she sell enough copies to cover the cost of publishing?

MEET MARK SALÓT

Basic Information:

✓ Male, aged 25–45.

✓ Lives in a rural area.

✓ In business 4 years.

✓ Annual business revenue of $225,000.

✓ Develops new services, products or message to keep clients coming back.

✓ Has multiple levels of services.

✓ Attends industry conferences to network and gain more visibility.

✓ Is within 30–45 days of making a decision about which publisher to work with.

Goals and Aspirations:

✓ Knows his audience.

✓ Is passionate about his topic and convinced that it's worthwhile and will help others.

✓ Loves to dig deeper into his area of expertise.

✓ Is intellectually curious and values learning.

✓ Enjoys the writing process and is committed to sharing what he knows.

✓ Values building his sphere of influence through networking and social media.

- ✓ Recognizes that a book is a means to achieve a higher quality of life for himself and his family.
- ✓ Recognizes that it's beneficial to have the right people doing the right jobs.
- ✓ Seeks to break through to the next level and is intent on getting it right.
- ✓ Is excited about writing a book, but doesn't want to participate more than necessary in the publishing process.

Information Sources:

- ✓ Reads trade journals and industry news sites.
- ✓ Follows Mike Michalowicz.
- ✓ Follows Russell Brunson.
- ✓ Watches Shark Tank.

Challenges:

- ✓ Has at least 1,000 followers across all platforms, but recognizes the need for a larger following.
- ✓ Wants to 10x his following.

Pain Points:

- ✓ It's not the best use of his gifts and talents to try to figure out publishing on his own.
- ✓ He is so passionate about this book that it's almost driving him mad that he can't get it done faster.

Objections to Sale:

- ✓ He doesn't want to change what he's written.

When you have a solid brainstormed list of ideal customers, you'll be able to quickly and easily create as many avatars as you need, yet still feel assured that each avatar represents a customer you'd enjoy working with.

As you continue to grow your business and expand your readership, remember to refine your brainstormed list by adding new characteristics and deleting ones that no longer work for you.

Don't Be Afraid to Go After the Niches

One of the concerns people often raise about creating a customer avatar is that it provides too narrow a view of their ideal client. What they're missing, though, is that there will still be many people who fit that description, even when they're as detailed as possible.

And the more focused you can make your topic, the better off you are.

If you're writing a book on mastering social media, selecting a specific platform to focus on will help draw the attention of readers interested in learning more about that particular platform. But someone in marketing would use that platform, whichever one it is, differently from an artist. So, writing a book on "How to Get the Most Out of Instagram for Photographers" would quickly enable potential readers to determine if that book was right for them. Are they a photographer? Are they interested in Instagram?

Being able to define your reader at that level makes it easier to determine the scope of your book as well. For example, a book for photographers should probably include sections on the best lenses, settings and filters to use when taking photographs, which a more casual user of Instagram would be less interested in.

The Money Is in the Niches

We have found that the more we cater to the niches, the easier it is to sell books. And if you're using your book to build a business, it becomes easier to identify eager prospects. Casting a wide net does not work well when using a book to build a business. If your business truly is suitable for a larger audience, you'd be better off writing a series of books, all based on a similar premise with modifications targeting specific readers.

Using our Instagram example above, you might create a series of books covering similar content but different readers. For example:

- ✓ "How to Get the Most Out of Instagram for Marketers"
- ✓ "How to Get the Most Out of Instagram for Speakers"
- ✓ "How to Get the Most Out of Instagram for School Systems"
- ✓ "How to Get the Most Out of Instagram for Baby Boomers"
- ✓ ...and more.

You might find that 70% of the content is the same across all the books in the series, but that other 30% allows you to speak to a specific reader and grab their attention.

Our best-selling titles are on exceedingly niche topics

At the end of 2018, the best-selling titles in our catalog at Emerald Lake Books were about exceedingly niche topics. One was a book on omni-channel retail, which I had never even heard of until my first conversation with the author, and another is a book written for people who want to raise pastured poultry in their backyards.

We'll talk a bit more about each of those later in this book. But the main message I want to get across here is this: don't be afraid to write a book that is purposely aimed toward a limited audience.

It is actually much easier to sell, because readers will be able to tell right away whether or not it is for them. If you don't have a backyard or you're not into the idea of raising your own chickens, you probably won't be interested in stress-free chicken tractor plans. (Unless you want to find out what chicken tractors are!)

You Can Always Expand Later

Even if you decide that your book will have a wider audience, I encourage you to create these customer avatars so your marketing can be written in a way that connects with them. You can always create more avatars and marketing plans along the way.

Know Your Ideal Reader

WHEN IT COMES TO YOUR BOOK, we recommend an exercise that's similar to defining your customer avatar. Except this time we emphasize the need to be very aware of who your ideal reader is. If you have a clear picture of your ideal reader as you're working, it allows you to write specifically for them.

For nonfiction authors, it also allows you to have a clear vision of the transformation you want to create for them.

If you've ever read about writing sales copy, you may have heard of something called a "transformation ladder" or a "path of transformation." Imagine your reader at the start of their journey. Your book would cover the 3 to 5 steps or milestones required to reach the outcome they want to secure for themselves. These are represented by the rungs of the transformation ladder.

You need to have a clear vision of where they are and what they want to achieve in order to define a precise roadmap for their path of transformation.

Whether you're writing fiction or nonfiction, though, knowing your ideal reader also ensures that your writing style naturally becomes more conversational toward them, instead of one-sided. And that makes for a much more engaging book for a reader to enjoy.

It also makes it much easier for the reader to determine whether your book is for them. You'll save prospective readers time and money if they can determine up front whether they are part of your target audience.

One of the simplest exercises we have found for this was introduced to us by our friend Justin Spizman. Justin is both a ghostwriter and a book architect (justinspizman.com), and he uses this "Dear Reader" exercise with his clients to help them clarify who their book is for at the beginning of the writing process.

We have since adapted and expanded his exercise for our own clients.

Dear Reader Exercise

The Dear Reader exercise consists of writing a letter to a prospective new reader. In the letter, you want to provide answers to the following questions:

1. Who are you?
2. What is this book about?
3. What inspired you to write it?
4. Who will it help?
5. Why are you the expert on this topic?
6. What makes your book unique?
7. What promise are you going to make the reader?

Of course, these questions are geared more toward nonfiction authors. They don't work quite as well when your book's primary aim is entertainment. So, we have a separate set of questions we ask our fiction authors to focus on answering in their letters.

1. Who are you?
2. What is this book about?
3. What inspired you to write it?
4. Why do you love this story?
5. What do you hope the reader will enjoy most about it?
6. What promise are you going to make the reader?

Whether you're a fiction or nonfiction author, write the letter as if you're speaking directly to that reader, using the first and second person ("I" and "you").

The completed letter should only be 2–3 pages long, but it will help you gain clarity regarding the outcome you want for your reader.

Keep in mind, this is not a questionnaire. This is a letter you're writing to a prospective reader. In it, you want to create a connection that demonstrates you know who they are and what their needs are, as well as why your book is the answer to what they're seeking. This is where you make it clear that you are the right guide for the transformation they want to achieve.

Typically, the flow of the letter initially establishes the core concepts you'll cover and how they're applicable to the reader. That's followed with a bit about who you are and why you're the best guide for them. For nonfiction authors, this often involves a compelling story that shares how you discovered the information yourself and how it changed your life. However, for fiction authors, it's more often an explanation of why you love the story so much.

After that, you'll want to set forth the unique selling proposition (or "USP" in business terms) that differentiates this book from others the reader could choose to read instead. Finally, the letter is wrapped up with a promise to your reader. Tell them what they can expect as a result of investing their time and money reading your book and putting what you share into practice.

If you have a coach or someone you trust who can provide you with honest feedback, we recommend sharing the letter with them. You want to hone and refine the letter until you're really clear about who the book is for and why this particular book will benefit them. Your promise to the reader, should they invest their time and money in you, has to resonate as something that particular reader will truly want. Getting feedback from a trusted source for this refining process is crucial.

When it's done, it should be easy to connect the dots—for example, a specific reader has a unique problem that you have demonstrated expertise in solving. If they invest in your book and put into practice what you teach them, they are almost guaranteed their desired outcome.

If you find you want more help with this exercise, we are happy to guide you through the process and provide feedback on your Dear Reader letter. Simply book a time with us at elbks.com/reader-ex.

We encourage our authors to view this letter as a beacon that guides their writing. It should resonate with the belief that buying and reading your book is the best thing a reader can do for themselves. After all, if you don't believe it, then why should they?

If your book isn't living up to the promises of this letter, the gaps and inconsistencies will become readily apparent. It will also help you determine what fits within the scope of the book and what is extraneous material or plotlines that, while good, are unnecessary and clutter your writing.

Many authors tell us that they never really knew when their book was done. They could have continued writing and weren't clear as to whether they'd written too much or not enough. This exercise defines the boundaries for the book and makes it clear when it's complete.

At Emerald Lake Books, we share the Dear Reader letter with the editors who work on a given manuscript. This allows them to verify that the author has delivered on their promise to the reader as they are editing the manuscript.

It gives us the opportunity to ensure that the book is as strong as it can be. At the editing stage, there is still time to make changes, if necessary, to help the book achieve its intended purpose.

Just as it defines the book's scope for the author, the letter also serves as a barometer for the editor to confirm that the book is complete and ready for publication.

Another benefit of the Dear Reader letter is that some portions of it may work well in the book's introduction or as part of the back cover copy or book listing description. So, this letter is one we refer to regularly as we prepare a book for publication.

Let me show you an example. The letter that follows is the one I wrote to you before I even began writing this book.

Sample Dear Reader Letter (Nonfiction)

Dear Reader,

If you've picked up this book to read, my guess is that you realized there's more to a book than just the number of copies sold.

Many publishers and pundits seem to think that the success of a book rests solely on its sales rank.

But if you're like most readers I know, it's not the sales rank that has impacted your decision to read this book. It's what you hope to get out of reading it that guides your decision.

When you were browsing the bookshelf or scrolling through Amazon, you had a specific need or desire that you were trying to fulfill. And something about this book made you wonder... *Could this be the one? Is the answer I need in here?*

It might have been the snazzy cover design or the engaging book description. Perhaps it was the number of reviews, the celebrity foreword or the caliber of endorsements.

Whatever your reason for picking up this particular book, here's what you'll get if you read it.

You'll learn to see a book, perhaps even your book, as a tool.

Like many tools, it can serve multiple purposes.

A hammer can pound a nail or draw one out. It can be used to pry things open or apart. It can be used to hook larger objects and move them elsewhere, or smash things to pieces.

Books can serve many purposes too. And that's what this particular book that you're holding in your hands is about. It's about making your book a multi-function tool that serves three distinct purposes.

1. It's about creating a book that edifies and inspires your readers. By the time they are done reading your book, their lives will be changed in some way. It might be a big change or a little one. But your reader will never be the same because what you wrote, what you had to say, mattered to them. It made a difference in their life, and that's going to cause them to want to share your book and the positive impact it had on them with others.

2. It's about using your book to grow your business or brand. I'll cover a number of different ways this can be accomplished in the next few chapters, like building your mailing list, establishing your expertise, finding more clients and booking more speaking engagements, to name a few. The success of a book should never be limited to the number of copies sold. There are other metrics that should be planned for, measured and understood, and it's often those "other metrics" that will have the most significant impact on you and your business.

3. Lastly, it's about making a difference in the world with what you have to share and what you've gained as a result. It's about recognizing that your success was only achievable with the support and effort of others, and now it's your turn to step up and do the same for someone else in a way that's uniquely yours.

When you craft a book that fulfills all three of these objectives, you are publishing with a purpose. And that's what *this* book is about—becoming purposeful about what you publish and how it's used.

As you read, you'll learn how to set genuine and authentic goals for your work that uplift your business and your reader, and make a positive difference in the world around you. You'll redefine what "success" means in terms of what you hope to accomplish, not how many copies you sell. And you'll chart a course in the right direction for achieving the goals you set.

Why am *I* the one to teach you this concept? Perhaps because it redefines how publishing is done. Purposeful publishing. Goal-oriented publishing. Whatever you want to call it. Up until this point, until I started talking about it, I've never heard any other person approach books in exactly this way. They may have strung together a few of the concepts, but I haven't seen anything as clearly articulated as this, until now.

These are the same steps I used to grow my own business when I first wrote *The Plan that Launched a Thousand Books*.

They're the same steps I've used with our publishing clients.

And they're the same steps I'm going to share with you within the pages of this book.

I grew up *loving* books. They were my escape, my safe haven in a home filled with great turmoil. They were also my classroom and playground. They made me braver than I believed, stronger than I seemed and smarter than I thought.

As I grew older, books have exposed me to more mentors than I could ever work with directly, allowing me to grow into the entrepreneur and human being I want to be. Any knowledge I could ever want is forever at my fingertips thanks to books. I can learn from experts who are popular today or sages who lived hundreds of years ago. And I can speak to experts who are yet to come through my own books.

It was only when I began sitting on the other side of the page, being the one to write all the words down for someone else to learn from and escape into, that I finally saw that being an author was so much more than just imparting knowledge. It was granting freedom, both to my reader as well as myself.

When I wrote books for my business, it spared me from having to work in close contact with people who didn't appreciate what I had to offer. By letting people experience my unique brand of expertise and humor, they could decide whether I was a good fit for them or not, without the pressure of my breathing down their neck or my having to endure the agony of cold-calling prospects.

Writing my books opened doors to speaking engagements, joint ventures, partner collaborations and other opportunities that organically grew my business. And this enabled me to attract clients who were a good fit to work with my company rather than going through the awkward cycle of pitching my services and hoping for a positive response.

I've taken everything I've learned about publishing with a purpose and included it in this book. I've pulled together case studies of how other people have used their books to achieve one or more of the uses outlined above and the impact that had on their business. I have also shared some of my own thoughts and experiences, drawn from my passion for teaching others and facilitating masterminds, as well as my ability to ask targeted questions to get people to dig deeper into themselves and what their goals are for their business.

My hope is to broaden your awareness of how powerful a book can be.

I can take a chisel and create the unskilled and rudimentary wood carvings I enjoy working on so much. But a master craftsman can take that same block of wood and the same chisel and create something so much more beautiful, simply because of their greater experience, superior knowledge and honed skill.

That's what makes this book unique.

You can find all sorts of books about how to write, how to write better, how to write faster, how to publish, how to market your book, how to game the system, how to launch a "bestseller," how to build a business, and on and on.

But what you won't find is a book about how to look at the message you want to share and package it in such a way that it becomes a multi-function tool in the hands of you, its master.

By the time you finish reading this book, you'll fall in love with writing all over again and you'll see the potential you have to change lives. You'll exchange the shackles of book sales figures for the accomplishment of the goals your specific book was designed to achieve. You'll be inspired by the success stories of other authors and filled with new ideas of how to create the outcomes you want most for your readers, your business and the difference you want to make in the world.

As you apply the lessons shared in this book to your own publishing efforts, success will build upon success.

It does not matter if the book you are writing is fiction or nonfiction. The business you are building may be a writing business, a brick-and-mortar business, a personal brand, or a products and services company. The principles are always the same.

Educate, entertain and inspire your readers.

Plan the outcomes you want to achieve, both for your readers and your business.

Implement the necessary components to accomplish those goals.

And when you've achieved the success you prepared for, share your good fortune with others and come back and tell me all about it so I can celebrate with you.

So, here's to taking the first step toward your next success.

Happy writing,
Tara R. Alemany

You may recognize some portions of this letter as you read through this book. A section was used in the Introduction, and other, smaller parts were worked into further areas as well. But the main thing I'd like you to notice is that I'm very clear about this book's purpose and why *I'm* the right person to be writing it.

When you write your own Dear Reader letter, you may find it difficult to convey why anyone should read your book. For some, it triggers their sense of "Imposter Syndrome" (a persistent internalized fear of being exposed as a fraud). To others, it may seem arrogant. But that's not the intent here.

The purpose is to demonstrate tempered confidence in your abilities and assure your reader that you know how to deliver what you've promised them. If you can't relay that information with confidence in your own abilities, how can you expect your reader to be confident in them?

Hopefully, since you're reading this book, my letter resonates with you, your desires and what you hope to get out of your reading. One of the benefits of having a Dear Reader letter written early in your writing process is that re-reading it as you write provides a surge of energy. It reconnects you to what you set out to do when you first started writing your manuscript. Every time I read this letter, I'm reminded of why I sacrificed the hours I could have spent with friends and family or "doing something fun" for the purpose of writing this book.

I know something that will benefit my readers. It will help them to be more focused and targeted with the books they write. Each book will serve a specific purpose, crafted by its author in a way that only they can do. And if I don't share what I know, if I keep my methods to myself, what good is my knowledge? Sharing it becomes one of the ways I can give back and make a difference in people's lives.

Sample Dear Reader Letter (Fiction)

Since the questions a fiction author must answer in their Dear Reader letter are different than for nonfiction authors, I wanted to provide an example of a letter for a fiction work as well, so you could see how it's done.

This letter was written by another of our authors, Esther Wallace, whom I've known since she was a 20-year-old. Her book, *The Savage War* (elbks.com/savage), was the first fiction novel published by Emerald Lake Books.

While we've been using our Publish with Purpose framework with nonfiction authors for awhile now, she was the first fiction writer to attempt any of these exercises. Thankfully, she understood what we were going for, and her Dear Reader letter demonstrates that.

Dear Reader,

I'm the author of *The Savage War*, which follows the first part of Arnacin's journey as he leaves his home on Enchantress Island to find a place he belongs and the fulfillment for which he yearns. When he agrees to help defend a kingdom against an enemy bent on hatred, his innocent assistance becomes harder than he ever imagined and he finds himself questioning the deepest of his childhood convictions.

This story derives mainly from my love of the complexities that make up human nature. Many of us have great dreams as children, and later find that those dreams are impractical. Sometimes, only hardships can teach us that honor is not in the laurel wreath, wealth is not in the money, and worth is not in our own worldwide popularity but in our close friendships.

Arnacin may not search for wealth, but he searches for honor and purpose in a world as regular as many people's day-to-day lives. His story is of growing up, of finding truth, and in that truth, finding all the things for which he yearned when young. I hope you empathize with that journey, and perhaps you will discover those things for yourself.

Although "growing up" stories are common, I felt that Arnacin's story was unique in the sense that he is, in his own way, both the protagonist and the antagonist of his story. It's his choices that bring about the end, good and bad, as I have often found that my own choices shape my life as well. If you are where he is in the Savage War, perhaps he'll be a companion to you as you face your own dragons.

May you prosper in your search.

Sincerely,
Esther Wallace

Note how she hit on all the relevant points: who she is, what the book is about, why she wrote it, what she loves about it, what she hopes the reader will enjoy, and how she anticipates reading it will affect them.

Based on this letter, we can assume that an ideal reader is someone who enjoys the complexities of human nature, especially as one is growing up and finding out that things aren't always as they seem, and who enjoys stories that remind us that sometimes we can even be our own worst enemy.

Align Your Topic with Your Avatar

In the previous chapter, we emphasize the importance of understanding who your ideal client or customer is. As mentioned, the people who buy your book are not necessarily always the same individuals who will read it. Many people do still buy books as gifts.

However, if you're writing your book to build your business or brand, you'll want to make sure that your business's ideal customer and your book's ideal reader are aligned.

CASE STUDY: AMY WALKER

A couple of years ago, I was talking with one of our business coaches, Amy Walker of Amy Walker Consulting (amywalkerconsulting.com). She is an executive business strategist, leadership expert, professional speaker and "sales guru."

At that time, she had a thriving business and loved what she was doing. Her ideal client was an entrepreneur, small business owner or individual involved in network marketing.

She began working on her new book and was excited by its content. She was very clear that her intended reader for the book was corporate trainers in mid- to large-sized companies. She saw this book as a great foundation for providing sales training to larger organizations, and thought it might even provide the opportunity for her to deliver some of those presentations herself.

After listening to her talk about her book for a little while, I had one question for her.

Was she looking to redefine her business?

Without understanding where the question came from, she replied that she was not. She loved working with her small business owners.

After conversing a little longer, she realized that the book she was writing was a book her ideal client would likely never need or use. And she had no interest in changing the direction or focus of her business.

Was she capable of providing sales training to large corporations? Certainly!

But that wasn't what was going to make her happy in the long run, and it would have pulled her away from working with the people she enjoyed working with most.

This is why it's so important to have a clear understanding of who your ideal client is, as well as who your target reader is. When you're writing a business-building book, if your vision of your client and reader aren't the same, you run the risk of growing a business you don't even want.

I ran into the same issue a couple of years ago. My first book, *The Plan that Launched a Thousand Books*, was first released as an eBook in 2012. It provides authors with a guide to creating their book marketing plan. Within two years, enough of the content was outdated that I decided to update it and release a second edition. That book was released in October 2014 as both eBook and paperback and marked the launch of my publishing company, Emerald Lake Books.

Two years later, I started work on a third edition of the book. There were new tools, techniques and processes I wanted to add to the book, and I'd lined up new endorsers and someone to write a foreword. However, as I discussed the updates with my partner, Mark Gerber, we realized that the book itself was mostly aimed at DIYers, who weren't our ideal customers since they weren't likely to want our publishing services.

The people we wanted to attract where those who viewed their book as an investment in their business, and who were willing to pay for professional help to produce and position a quality book that would accomplish specific goals for their business.

As a result, work on the third edition of *The Plan that Launched a Thousand Books* was halted and we began laying the groundwork for the book you're currently reading, *Publish with Purpose*.

Sometimes authors will write whatever we're passionate about at the time, without really weighing it against what we want to accomplish. It's not always easy to see that ourselves. You may notice that in both Amy's case and my own, neither of us recognized how off-target we were until we discussed it with someone we trusted.

It's a useful means of testing our concept to see if it hits its mark or falls short. But it's also a necessary part of ensuring that when we publish with purpose, we stay on track.

If you find yourself struggling to decide whether your book idea will help you attract the readers and clients you want, you may want to explore this opportunity to work with me at elbks.com/VIPcall.

Know What You Want to Achieve

A BIG PART OF PUBLISHING YOUR BOOK with purpose is understanding the goals you have in mind for it. You need to know what you want it to achieve for your reader as well as your business, and what you want the book's overall impact to be.

By the end of the last chapter, if you did the exercises, you should have a fairly clear picture of what you want your book to achieve for your reader. Hopefully, you've also been able to confirm that your book's content is aligned with the needs of your ideal client or customer. If you haven't, now is the time to make adjustments.

But if you're ready to move on, the next goal we focus on is what you want the book to achieve for your business.

Before we get there though, I want to clarify that, even if you are not an entrepreneur or a business owner, you do still have a business.

Every author owns a business. Your product is your book. Your product is your message. In order to be successful, you have to think about your book as an item that needs to be publicized, marketed and sold.

If you're not convinced of that, consider this. Most tax authorities throughout the world expect you to report the income from your book sales, so they can appropriately tax you.

If the tax authorities consider your writing as a business, it's about time you think of it that way as well. So consult your tax accountant to work out how best to approach this issue in your country.

Let's use the U.S. as an example, though, so you can see what I mean here. If your writing business is run properly, you'll be able to deduct expenses against your income. This will help you retain more of your money rather than giving it all to Uncle Sam. But either way, he wants his share, so you may as well start thinking about it as a business!

If you don't, the income from your writing will be taxed as "ordinary income." Which means the tax you owe is based on your total income. When you declare your writing venture as a business, though, it's business income, and any expense you incur to generate that income is deducted from the total *before* tax is calculated.

Here are two examples that demonstrate the impact of that tiny distinction, based on the 2019 U.S. tax tables. Let's say you earned $100,000 in income as a result of your writing, and you had $25,000 in expenses.

Hobby	Business
Earnings: $100,000 Tax Rate: 24% Taxes Due: $18,289.50 Expenses: $25,000 Net: $56,710.50	Earnings: $100,000 Expenses: $25,000 Tax Rate: 22% Taxes Due: $12,439.50 Net: $62,560.50

In this scenario, claiming your writing income as part of a business, rather than ordinary income, would save you

$5,850 in taxes because the expenses are deducted before the taxes are calculated. This means you're taxed on less income. In this scenario, it even drops you into a lower tax bracket as well, meaning that *all* of your income is taxed less, not just the income from your business. So it's well worth having a conversation with your accountant about what makes the most sense for you.

A good resource for authors who are just starting out in business is Carol Topps' "Taxes for Writers" and other materials on her website (taxesforwriters.com).

That said, it's time for you to figure out what you want the book to accomplish for your business. We believe there is no single benefit to having a book for your business. In fact, there are many benefits. It's all about where your focus is and how you leverage it.

Like any other tool, your book will be as effective for you as you are at using it. If you simply publish it and do little else, then it's nothing more than a vanity project. But if you publish it and leverage it properly, it can accomplish great things for you.

When people consider whether a book is successful or not, they often focus on book sales. While that can certainly be one of the performance indicators that you monitor, it should not be the only one.

As an author, at a minimum, you should be seeking to grow your mailing list and securing more reviews.

It is generally agreed that "the money is in the [mailing] list." Adding subscribers to your mailing list means that they are granting you permission to continue to build a relationship with them.

Happy subscribers make future book launches that much easier. So give some thought to how you might further your relationship with your readers to ensure that they are eager to support you and purchase other products and services from you.

Securing more reviews is also important because it acts as social proof for your book. This ensures that a prospective reader who is unfamiliar with you has the benefit of hearing from other satisfied customers.

This kind of social proof will go a long way toward enabling you to sell your books to individuals beyond your friends and family.

The sad truth, though, is that most first-time authors have a limited platform to sell their book to. They end up tapping into their own personal network to sell their book. Selling to anyone who doesn't already know them becomes a major hurdle. The result is that most first-time authors never sell more than 250 copies of their book over its entire lifetime, according to the latest consensus. Even if you managed to earn an average of $5 per book sold, that's only $1,250 over the lifetime of your book.

So book sales are a poor performance indicator for many authors. And while the social proof of securing reviews will help clear the hurdle of selling to people who don't know you, it takes a significant number of book sales to make up for the time and effort spent to produce and promote it.

If you want your book to be profitable, you need to focus on something bigger than book sales. This is where understanding the transformation your reader wants to experience helps you identify the best means of marrying what you have to offer with the transformation the reader hopes to achieve. This ultimately enables you to use your book to build your business.

In giving your reader the necessary steps or directions to achieve their goals, you create an opportunity to accomplish multiple benefits for your business.

Common uses for a business-building book include:

✓ Generating leads.

✓ Encouraging engagement with your material.

✓ Establishing your expertise.

✓ Securing speaking engagements.

✓ Increasing your fees.

✓ Building a community.

✓ Creating passive income.

✓ Setting the record straight.

✓ And, of course, building your mailing list.

While a single book can accomplish all of these things, it's important to know which of them are your priorities when you're publishing it. This will dictate the offers you share with your readers and how you approach the launch and marketing of your book.

Educate, Inspire or Entertain

Sometimes a book's primary purpose is simply to educate, inspire or purely entertain readers. Histories, biographies, memoirs, children's books, fiction and so many other genres share this same goal.

After all, isn't that what *any* good book does? It educates, inspires or entertains. If it doesn't do at least one of those, it's probably *not* a good book! Even textbooks, self-help and business books all must hit on at least one of these to succeed.

However, when it's the primary purpose for the book, then the author's point in writing is to affect a change of some kind in the reader, whether that's to make them more knowledgeable, more capable or more relaxed.

When this is your main goal for your book, the way you're going to use it to build your business as a writer will be to encourage engagement with you and build anticipation for whatever you produce next. To do that, create a mailing list where people can subscribe to learn about the inner workings of your process, read deleted scenes or character sketches, receive exclusive bonus content, learn about books by other authors you think they might enjoy, or volunteer to be part of the launch team for your next book. Have them follow you on social media and be sure to start conversations with them and interact there.

Essentially, when you write a book that educates, inspires or entertains, you want to continue that experience with your reader even after the reader closes the covers of your book. If you inspire, then share inspirational posts or ask for reader favorites. If you educate, then share the latest news about your topic and how the subject continues to grow and evolve. And if you entertain, don't hesitate to share other titles (even from other authors) you think they might enjoy.

Build Your Mailing List = Generate Leads

At a minimum, every business-building book should provide opportunities for readers to join your mailing list. (You can join mine at elbks.com/newsletter.) This, in effect, becomes a way to generate leads that will help you sell future books, as well as ancillary products and services. But it also creates the opportunity for readers to prolong their reading enjoyment.

There are many different offers that will entice readers to join a mailing list. But when you understand what your reader is hoping to get out of reading your book, then it makes it easier to settle on offers they will want.

The simplest way is to offer bonus materials from within the book. For example, you could provide downloadable templates or worksheets, grant entry to a membership site, or a number of other things.

Another option we sometimes offer during our launches is to have people who purchased the printed book forward their receipt to a designated email address in order to receive the eBook version right away. The email address is set up with an auto-responder with instructions on how to download the eBook, so there's no manual intervention needed. Then we use Zapier to monitor the email address and create or update contact records in our CRM system for the addresses that contact us, and tag them in such a way that we know the contact has purchased the book.

Both of these methods enable us to capture email addresses of readers, even if they didn't purchase the book directly from us.

You can also participate in BookFunnel promotions, where you join with other authors who share a similar audience and collectively promote free downloads of a collection that includes your book for a limited-time giveaway. Whenever anyone downloads your book, they are required to provide an email address, and you can configure the offer in such a way that they can opt to join your mailing list at the same time, if they'd like.

Another popular method of building your mailing list while also increasing the visibility of your book is to make a "Free+-Shipping" offer. That's when you offer your printed book for free, plus the cost of shipping. Typically, the "shipping" fee is $7.95. But when you break down the numbers, this fee is actually covering the cost of both printing and shipping.

In the U.S., for example, Media Mail currently costs $2.75 for packages up to 1 lb., and $3.27 for up to 2 lbs. (This is a mailing class that is cheaper and usually slower than first-class mail, but commonly used for mailing books and other types of media.) Based on that, most book mailings are going to cost $3.27 or less. If your new reader has spent $7.95 to get a "free" copy of your book and you incur a fairly standard 3.99% merchant fee for processing the payment, then you still have $4.36 left over after shipping the book. For many books, that's enough to cover the print costs and still have enough to cover the shipping supplies. So, while it's likely a "wash" for the author financially, it is a fantastic way to get your book into the hands of many new readers, who are willing to give you their email address and mailing information in exchange for a copy of the book.

Encourage Engagement

You always want to be thinking about different ways to encourage engagement with you and your content, whether that's through social media or other methods that solidify the connection between the reader and your work.

A friend of mine, Mark Wayne Adams (mwa.company), is an amazing children's book author and illustrator. He's won numerous awards throughout his career and has illustrated dozens of books, including *The Fart Fairy series; Nicholas, that's Ridiculous; Parts of Speech Parade* and others. For many of these books, "bonus features" are offered, including coloring pages, craft projects, origami instructions, word searches, discussion guides and lesson notes. But one of the items that captured my attention most was the bonus that goes along with John Hope's *Frozen Floppies*.

The Floppies are these charming little donkeys who are trying to rescue their friends who have turned into frozen flopsicles.

Knowing his market, Mark understood that this book would typically be purchased by a grandparent or parent to read to a child they love. So, the bonus that was created for the book was a sewing pattern. That way, the child and a beloved adult could make their own stuffed Floppy together. Rather than going through the expense of licensing and creating merchandise themselves, they turned it into a bonding opportunity between a child and a loved one.

In this particular case, they didn't use it as an option for building their mailing list, although they could have. Instead, they had the pattern printed on the inside of the dust jacket—thereby making the hardcover version of the book more valuable to buyers. Then they encouraged readers to "Be social! Share Floppy photos using #MyFloppy."

In that way, they were able to get people to share on social media about their experiences with the book and how much kids loved their Floppies. This audience was willing to promote the book by using the hashtag simply because the book provided their family with sweet memories they cherished.

This is something we all should aspire to with our books. When we want people to be willing to share about our books, it shouldn't be about us. It should be about them and what the book has created for them or inspired them to do.

Establish Expertise

One of the greatest benefits of having a book is that it allows you to clarify your message. The process of writing compels you to find clear and straightforward ways to communicate your vision, but it also forces you to think about who your audience is and what their needs are. And when you can demonstrate an understanding of and connection with your reader, it provides them with a similar sense of connection with you. You "get" them. You know their needs. And most importantly, you care enough to help them.

It also prompts you to dig deeper into the topic you're writing about, which increases your familiarity with the subject matter and makes it easier for you to have ongoing conversations about it.

These conversations may include social media interactions, blog posts, podcasts, videos and other unique and creative ways of sharing your thoughts about the topic. The more closely connected your name becomes with the subject, the more likely you are to be perceived as an expert on it.

This means leveraging the fact that you're an author of a book on the topic to gain media attention, secure interviews, and strike up conversations with other experts in the field, who are now your peers.

While many authors will focus on trying to become an Amazon bestseller, there isn't much real value in that designation. Once you understand how Amazon's sales ranks work, it's simply a matter of doing the math to figure out how to game the system. Barring any surprises, you can often come away with a bestseller ranking or a "Hot New Release" designation during your launch period. But neither of these accurately reflect actual sales of the book. You can achieve an Amazon bestseller while having in fact sold only a handful of books. So we see it as a somewhat misplaced expenditure of energy when there are so many other worthwhile pursuits that will translate into success for you.

An alternative we often recommend to our authors is to pursue book award competitions run by respected organizations.

There are plenty of competitions out there that are purely popularity contests, and that's not the kind of book award we recommend trying to secure. Rather, we recommend submitting your book to award competitions where the judges are industry professionals, such as librarians and booksellers, or your industry peers, meaning people who are experts in your subject area.

Some of our favorites include:

- ✓ Reader's Favorite Book Awards.
- ✓ Florida Authors and Publishers Association's President's Book Awards.
- ✓ Independent Publisher Book Awards (IPPY).
- ✓ Axiom Business Book Awards.
- ✓ NextGen Indie Book Awards.
- ✓ IBPA's Benjamin Franklin Book Awards.

There are many quality award competitions out there. Of those listed above, all accept both fiction and nonfiction entries, including the Axiom Business Book Awards, which has a Business Fable category. So, don't make assumptions about a competition purely based on its name. Do your research to choose the right ones for you and the genre of your book.

The benefit of winning or placing in an award competition is that it counts as a professional social proof, which is great for marketing purposes.

Another way of generating social proof is to secure editorial reviews of your book. You can do that through organizations like Kirkus, BlueInk Reviews and Foreword Clarion. You can also approach celebrities and influencers for endorsements.

Each of these approaches provides an opportunity for someone else to validate your knowledge and expertise, while lending their name and influence to your work.

Case Study: Lionel Binnie

I mentioned earlier that one of our authors, Lionel Binnie, wrote a book on a very niche subject.

Prior to our first phone call, I had never even heard the phrase "omni-channel retail," which refers to a multichannel approach to sales that seeks to provide customers with a seamless shopping experience, whether they're shopping online from a desktop or mobile device, by telephone, or in a brick-and-mortar store.

It was Lionel's desire to become recognized as an expert in this area. He had a scholarly approach to consuming existing information about it, and easily synthesized the material to create unique and approachable ideas.

The biggest barrier to establishing his expertise was that he had a very limited platform.

When I evaluated existing books on the subject, I realized that the majority of books available were either textbooks or had poorly conceived covers and descriptions.

The first step in establishing Lionel's expertise was to ensure that his book, *The Future of Omni-Channel Retail: Predictions in the Age of Amazon* (elbks.com/omnichannel), was easily discoverable and that it was perceived as being approachable and authoritative. This involved doing competitive research as well as applying search engine optimization to the book's title, subtitle and listing description.

Using information gathered during the competitive research, we compiled a list of keywords potential readers might be using to search for books related to our author's topic. Even before the book was released, we began running Amazon (AMS) ads to target those keywords and ensure the discoverability of this book.

The next step was to make sure that authority was lent to the author through an endorsement from a well-known industry leader. Paco Underhill, author of the *New York Times* bestseller *Why We Buy* and founder and CEO of Envirosell, Inc., provided an endorsement that is prominently displayed on the book's cover, as well as in the listing description.

The combination of the prominent visibility and influencer endorsement helped position our author as an expert on his subject matter. The result has been that he has received speaking invitations from a variety of organizations and universities, as well as letters from readers all around the world.

Within the first six months, his book was adopted by the marketing programs at multiple universities. Small marketing firms and the marketing departments of larger companies purchased bulk copies of the book for their entire staff. And a major food retailer reached out to him to ask if he would speak to their organization.

With no real platform to begin with, this author has established himself as an expert in his topic, and he is being sought out by people who need his knowledge and expertise to help them address the problems they are facing. To facilitate this learning further, he has established a new website to continue connecting with his readers and exploring the ever-changing needs of commerce. (Visit discoveromniretail.com to learn more.)

Essentially, this book has taken his business to the next level in its growth, simply because of how easily it established his expertise.

This is what Lionel had to say about the whole experience:

> Through the process of writing the book, I have clarified my expertise and distilled my ideas, not just for my readers, but for myself as well. It's also revealed adjacent topic areas for me to explore. So writing with the intent to publish clarifies one's mind, integrates one's thinking and, even, makes one grow as a person.
>
> Creativity is an exploration of self-identity and meaning, in and of itself. The pressure of writing something that you want and expect others to read makes one try harder. In other words, you dig deeper and think harder because you know others will read it. It's different than just journaling for personal interest, for example.

Secure Speaking Engagements

Just as writing a book helps to establish your expertise, it can also help you secure speaking engagements. As mentioned earlier, the process of writing helps you to clarify your message. It makes you dig deep and think long and hard about what it is you want to share. This process helps you to be a better speaker. It prepares you to answer questions extemporaneously, to engage in conversations with well-wishers, and to hold your own with influencers and expert peers.

I've often heard it said that if an event planner is considering two speakers of equal caliber who talk on the same subject, the one with the book is the one they are more likely to hire.

Unfortunately, these days, it seems like everyone has a book. That's why we don't recommend stopping at your book launch. Elevate your book to the next level. Ensure that you have done the work necessary to stake a claim on the description "award-winning book." Or, if you want to be able to stake a claim on "best-selling book," ensure that your launch and marketing plan accounts for becoming a best-selling book where it counts, like the *New York Times*, *Wall Street Journal*, *USA Today* or another list relevant to your target audience.

If speaking engagements are part of what you want your book to accomplish for your business, make sure that you're clear about the role speaking plays in your business.

When I was getting started speaking at busines, writing and publishing conferences, I based all of my talks on the content of one of my books. It was a natural lead-in that prompted attendees to purchase my book when I was finished speaking. Whatever talk I had just given gave them a high-level overview of the material they could find in more detail in my book.

There are many ways to repurpose content. Using the material in your book to supply the subject matters for your presentations is simply one of them. But just as establishing Lionel's expertise through his book led to speaking engagements, speaking engagements reinforce the impression of expertise, and both are bound up in the wrapper of a book.

If you want your book to generate speaking engagements, you have to be willing to make it known in the book that you are a speaker. This means finding a balance between stating the fact and avoiding sounding pretentious or boastful.

Take a look at how I did that three paragraphs above. I didn't make a big deal about being a speaker, but I worked it into the material by simply stating it as a fact and sharing a tip you could use based on what works for me. Yet, I'm also clear about the types of conferences I was speaking at, which helps give clear context for suitable speaking engagements for me, should someone want to invite me to speak. It was simple, matter-of-fact and clear, and that's what you should strive for too. Don't over-share. Don't repeat it too often. But make it known and plant a seed for the reader that they might be able to have you come speak to their organization or at their favorite conference.

Another, more direct, way to secure speaking engagements from your book is to end your author bio with a call to action. Invite readers to contact you if they'd be interested in having you speak at their next event and tell them how to do that. Alternatively, you can provide a website address where they can learn more about you as a speaker, as well as how to hire you.

Increase Fees

As your perceived expertise grows, so does your influence. And when you secure more speaking engagements, the demand for your services will likely increase.

Over time, these outcomes will allow you to increase the fees you charge for your products and services. But first, people must be aware of the services or products you offer, beyond just your book.

In addition, as you leverage the visibility your book will bring, there may be opportunities for joint ventures with your peers or other influencers. As you "level up" by "playing with the big boys," the perceived value of working with you directly will increase, enabling you to command greater fees.

When it comes to increasing your fees, the most important thing is to recognize that your mindset plays a huge role in valuing your worth. We often don't judge ourselves fairly. The work we choose to do, we typically do because it comes naturally to us. As a result, we think of it as "easy" and therefore not worth paying a lot of money for.

That couldn't be farther from the truth. The people who are willing to hire you are doing so because they struggle to do that work themselves or because doing it themselves takes time away from the things that come easily and naturally to them. As a result, they place great value on what you have to offer. And while you don't want to price yourself out of the market, if you charge too little, they will perceive the value of what you have to offer as being lesser.

Understand that they need what you have. As a result, you should charge what is fair for the expertise you have to offer. Don't diminish your value in the eyes of potential clients by charging too little for your services.

Instead, consider what your value is to them. If your products or services free your readers to spend more time on the things they are best at or alleviate a problem for them, there is great value in that.

Put yourself in their shoes. What would it be worth to you to have a bothersome chore, worrisome task or painful problem easily fixed by someone else? What would it be worth to you if you had extra hours you could spend with your family and friends or on your business growth?

That's the perspective you need to adopt in order to price your products and services in a way that's honest and authentic.

Create Partnership Opportunities

Most authors want to establish their expertise so that it's easier for potential clients to find and work with them. However, a side benefit of establishing your expertise is that other influencers may be open to partnership opportunities with you.

Such opportunities can take many forms. Perhaps it's conducting a webinar or course together. Or creating a podcast or live event for your shared audience.

You can even put a slight twist on the idea of having a niche audience for your book by co-authoring a version of your message that targets a more specific demographic. This is a highly effective way to take your message and make it desirable to the masses, one audience at a time.

A great example of how this is done is Hal Elrod's book, *The Miracle Morning* (elbks.com/miraclemorning). Since the book came out in 2012, eleven additional books have been added to the series. Each one has been co-authored with one or more other individuals to expand the original concept to apply to a smaller audience. The co-authors are chosen because these niche audiences are "their people." Having their name on the book means that they'll promote it to their audience at the same time as creating visibility for Hal and his message. Thus far, the series builds on his message and shows how it applies to real estate agents, salespeople, network marketers, writers, parents and families, entrepreneurs, those experiencing relationship difficulties, college students, millionaires and addicts.

In Hal's case, the first book in the series, *The Miracle Morning*, sells the most copies on a consistent basis, but the other books provide additional buying options for readers, and contribute to the overall popularity of his message. And the reworked, niche versions provide him with the opportunity to co-author the subsequent books in the series to leverage other people's knowledge and expertise with the target audience.

Build a Community

There are many ways a community can be built around a book's ideas and concepts. You can create a Facebook group, inviting readers to connect with each other and share experiences as they apply what they've learned. You can add discussion questions to the end of your book to facilitate book clubs and other groups of readers enjoying and discussing the book together. You can create a group coaching program or membership site that provides readers with an opportunity to work directly with you in a group environment. Or perhaps your book lends itself to a mastermind format, Meetup group or a live action role-playing (LARPing) game.

Part of building a community around your book is to return to your Dear Reader letter and think about the needs of that ideal reader. How can you use the material from your book to create an extension of it that appeals to your reader and connects them to a community?

This is something you'll typically want to have thought through before the book's publication, so you can take the necessary steps to create the foundation for the group. That's not to say you can't create group opportunities later, but if it's done beforehand, it can be referenced in the book, making it easier for the reader to discover other ways to engage with you and your content.

Passive Income

Of course, one of the enviable things about having a business-building book is the potential to create a passive income for yourself.

The most obvious source of that passive income would come from book sales themselves. But when you consider printing costs and royalty shares, you may only see a few dollars from the sale of each book. You won't build a financial empire based on book sales alone.

However, it's not unreasonable to offer related products or services in your book to those who are interested. And it's not uncommon to see a book funnel that starts with the sale of the book and leads to an increase in podcast listeners (good for branding and advertising revenue) or the sale of a course, a group coaching program, related merchandise or a workshop series. It can even lead to one-on-one VIP coaching.

Passive income can come from many sources, but the best way to generate it is to make sure that you have a clear funnel defined that maps out the reader's journey from reading your book to buying your products and services, if you have any. And that starts with defining a "value ladder."

A value ladder maps out your products and services visually, in ascending order of value and price. Customers can engage with you at any point on the ladder, but it enables you to have a clear understanding of the value that must be offered (the solution to a problem) in order to guide a customer to the next rung (higher priced offering) of the ladder.

Once you've defined your value ladder, you can set up a book funnel that leads readers from the book into other parts of the funnel with free content in between that brings them closer to their goals.

All of that can be set up to run seamlessly on auto-pilot using a good automated marketing campaign system. This leaves your time and energy free to focus on the high-ticket items that require your participation to justify the price.

Based on the reader's responses to offers in the funnel, the automated campaign can be defined to identify a suitable upsell (more expensive item) or downsell (less expensive item), so your reader is always presented with material that's useful and relevant to their particular needs.

While it takes planning and time to develop more complex funnels, the passive income opportunities are there when you stay focused on the most important thing: the transformation your reader wants to make in their own life. Keep the products and services you're offering relevant to them and their needs, and they will continue to buy from you.

And don't make the mistake of thinking that this only applies to nonfiction books. Value ladders can be built for fiction books as well. For instance, when a reader completes the first book in a series, it's fairly common to have the next book in the series offered at the end of the first. That in itself represents a (very flat) ladder. But if the reader purchased that second book in, say, a six-book series, you could follow it up with a special offer to buy the remaining four books as a bundle at a discounted price.

CASE STUDY: JOHN SUSCOVICH

Unlike Lionel, whom we discussed earlier, John Suscovich of Farm Marketing Solutions (farmmarketingsolutions.com) came to us in 2016 with a very large existing platform of over 35,000 followers. (By the end of 2019, he will have over 100,000 subscribers on YouTube, which is his primary channel to connect with people.)

John is the author of *Stress-Free Chicken Tractor Plans* (elbks.com/chickens), which we mentioned earlier when we discussed writing for the niches. While a book on building chicken tractors is a very niche subject, he has used it to build his mailing list, add to his YouTube subscribers and generate additional sales. Each of these ultimately led into additional sources of passive income.

The book itself teaches people how to build their own mobile backyard chicken coops based on a design John developed. It's now commonly referred to as a "Suscovich tractor." (How's that for establishing expertise and recognition?)

At the end of his book, John acknowledges that information changes quickly these days. He suggests that readers may want to visit his website for updated information, such as links to his favorite poultry books and favorite resources, more videos from his farm, free PDF downloads on topics like troubleshooting diseases and the results of various experiments he performs on the farm.

He also invites his readers to be part of something bigger— an initiative he started to encourage people to grow their own pastured poultry and "taste the difference." As he writes in his book, "I got into pasture-based systems for the politics and I stayed for dinner."

He makes sure people are aware of his podcast and his YouTube channel, as well as his eight-week video course on raising broiler chickens from start to finish. Obviously, if you're going to take the time to build chicken tractors, you might be interested in resources that help you to do so effectively. And for those who are approaching pastured poultry with a business orientation, he offers resources for growing your pastured broiler operation as well.

Overall, no matter what your reason for building a Suscovich tractor, John's book teaches you how to do so. He offers you the additional resources you need to be successful at raising chickens as a small-scale operation, like in your backyard, whether they're for personal or business use.

These additional resources enable readers to connect with John in the way that's most comfortable for them. And whether they choose to purchase one of those resources now or engage with him through one of his free channels, he's able to continue the relationship with them once they have finished reading his book.

And because John has taken the time to understand the unique needs of his ideal reader, he's able to anticipate their future needs. In the end, this book funnel positions him as a trusted advisor to his readers.

The fun thing for Emerald Lake Books, as his publisher, is that we got to enjoy his excitement when he found his book holding its own on the same bookshelf as his idols soon after it was published.

> Thanks to [Emerald Lake Books], I am on the same page on Amazon as many of my idols. The "I got into this career because of this person" kind of people. Having my book published is bringing my business to a new level and I look forward to the next book project with ELB.

Set the Record Straight

On rare occasion, we come across a book whose purpose isn't so much to build a business as to shed light on an incident with the sole intention of setting the record straight. For this type of project, the book serves as a platform for a voice to be heard that might not otherwise be listened to.

Such was the case for another of our authors, Jack Stetson (elbks.com/stetson).

Publish with Purpose

CASE STUDY: JACK STETSON

Jack's step-grandfather, John Leahy, was the last owner and general manager of a regional fair in Connecticut called the "Great Danbury State Fair." It began officially operating in 1869 and ran on a regular schedule (10 days every year) until 1981.

In 1962, a nonprofit foundation was established to manage the Fair after John was gone. Slowly, but steadily, he transferred shares of the Fair into this charitable foundation until it owned more than half of the Fair. That's when a bomb dropped. The foundation had not been properly set up to carry on the business of the Fair. John was forced to have the Fair stock appraised and had to buy back all the shares he'd donated.

Unfortunately, by the time that was all done, he never got around to determining how to safeguard the longevity of the Fair in a more suitable manner. So, when he died in 1975, nothing was in place to protect the Fair itself, and the property the Fair was held on was counted as part of his estate.

As one of John's heirs, Jack, of course, stood to benefit when John's estate was settled. But what wasn't clear to the public at the time was that Jack was an heir to the estate, not a trustee of it. And the trustees had a fiduciary responsibility to handle John's estate in a way that would result in the most money for its heirs.

The problem was, the fairground property was in a prime location, along an interstate that regularly saw traffic from both New York and Connecticut. And even though Jack loved the Fair and wanted nothing more than to continue operating it as his family had done since he was a boy, the trustees of John's estate had a fiduciary responsibility to sell the ground out from under it.

Therefore, one evening in 1981, Jack was informed by the trustees that a buyer had exercised their option to purchase the property. He had no say in the matter, but when the news hit the papers in the morning, a hue and a cry went up. Since he was the face of the Fair, he was accused of being greedy and self-centered for ending the beloved Fair and selling the grounds to a mall developer. To this day, there are still fans of the Fair who will not set foot in the Danbury Fair Mall that now stands in its place, and plenty of people who are still upset with Jack.

So, it was important to Jack that people understood the whole story, not just the sensationalized parts that weren't even true.

When Jack's grandmother passed away in 1982, he found a manuscript in her attic that chronicled the history of the Fair up to 1955. When he retired, Jack decided to complete the remaining years of the history and seize the opportunity to finally set the record straight, all while providing readers with a wonderful history of the Fair they all knew and loved.

No expense was spared in the production of *The Life and Times of the Great Danbury State Fair* (elbks.com/danburyfair). At 312 pages with 177 photographs spanning the history of the Fair, the book serves as a wonderful tribute to an annual tradition that people still remember with love.

The book was crafted with all the affection and care befitting its subject. It was intended to be a way of honoring the Fair and remembering the good times, and readers have received it that way. As the only account of the Fair's history that was written by the owner's family, it provides an intimate insider's view while providing a platform for Jack to share how the demise of the Fair really came about.

Finally, the record has been set straight.

CLAIM YOUR SUCCESS

FOR SOME AUTHORS, CRAFTING A BOOK to meet a specific purpose may feel manipulative or unnatural. That's not what you're going for here. All of your writing should be done in such a way that it provides tremendous value for your ideal reader.

I was having a conversation with a sales coach once. During it, I complained that I hate selling. To pitch my services to someone feels slimy to me. It doesn't come naturally and really makes me uncomfortable.

This coach asked me what I liked best about my work. It was very easy for me to get excited about the fact that the business I have built is one that uses my natural gifts and talents. I truly enjoy what I do.

He then asked me if I thought people benefited from using my services. Since it was easy for me to see how I make a difference for my clients, it was a simple question to answer. Yes!

The final question had me scratching my head. Wasn't I doing people a disservice if they had a problem my services could solve and I didn't tell them about it?

The key was simply to recognize who was wrestling with a problem my services could solve. By telling *those* individuals how their lives could be easier, I was alleviating a burden they were wrestling with. It wasn't a hard sell—it was a lifeline. And for those who are tired of fighting with the problem, the solution was easy to embrace. Work with me.

Know What You Want to Accomplish

It's the same thing for your book. Don't hold anything back. Provide the reader with all the value you can. Make it clear you understand why they are reading the book and what they're hoping to get out of it. But then let them know you are there for them.

Give them ways to connect with you outside the book. And I don't mean just how to follow you on social media. I mean, how to *learn* more from you. How to work with you. How to implement what they've learned in the book. How to solve the problem that made them pick up the book in the first place.

This is why it is so important to understand who your ideal reader is and why they have chosen to read your book. If it's purely for entertainment, make sure you entertain them. And then follow that up by letting them know how they can find other sources of entertainment you've created or enjoyed.

If they've chosen to read your book to solve a problem, make sure you clearly defined that problem and how to solve it. Then think about similar problems they may be experiencing. If your book covers the technical aspects of how to build a website, your reader may also want more information about how to write great content or find good stock images or select a hosting service. So think about other ways you can support them in solving the issue they're facing.

Always provide value.

If you do, it's not unreasonable to make offers that enable your reader to connect further with you. As a matter of fact, if you want to stay in business, it likely depends on you being able to create as much visibility for yourself as you can. That means doing things like growing your mailing list, having more conversations with people, and making sure people know what it is you do and what you have to offer.

After all, if you go out of business, all those people whose problems you can solve will be left to figure things out on their own.

So as you write your book, consider where, when and how it makes sense to provide your readers with additional ways to connect with you. Sometimes, in the midst of a chapter, a specific resource you created might be of value. It's okay to tell them about it and how to get it. Don't be shy. If it's going to help them, let them know about it.

You may have noticed I did this myself, when I offered the opportunity to work directly with me on your Dear Reader letter. Keep it natural and don't stress about it. If it will benefit your reader, don't let discomfort or uncertainty cause you to keep it a secret from them.

Other times, you may want to share it as a special offer displayed in an ad at the back of the book. That's okay too.

The main thing is to make sure that the book does not become a pitch fest. Readers will see right through that. So, the offers you make must be legitimate and of value to the reader where and when you make them.

This is where the next stage of our goal-setting framework comes in. You need to know what your priorities are for this particular book in building your business or brand. With all of the different options we covered in the last chapter, there are plenty of opportunities to build your business. But what is most important for this specific book?

Here's where another exercise can help. It's something we developed for our own authors and it's based on a concept similar to the Dear Reader exercise we described earlier. However, where the Dear Reader exercise helps the author and editor ensure that the content of the book delivers on the promise the author is making to the reader, the Dear Author exercise helps the author and marketer make sure the book's purpose as a business-building tool is clearly defined. In turn, this helps identify the right marketing and publicity opportunities for what you hope to achieve.

Dear Author Exercise

We affectionately refer to the Dear Author exercise as a "verbal vision board." When we make that connection for people, they grasp the concept much more quickly. However, instead of pasting pictures on a board, you're going to write another letter—this time, it's from your future self and it's being written to encourage the "you" you are today.

Many first-time authors are stunned to find that writing the book is the easy part. The hard work begins once the book is published, and it needs to be marketed and promoted in order for readers to find it. So this letter is intended to give you a vision of how all that hard work will pay off for you and what that would look like to the world at large.

By embracing the potential of that vision, it helps you connect with what best-selling author and speaker Simon Sinek refers to as your "why" (startwithwhy.com). In his book, *Start with Why* (elbks.com/startwithwhy), he sagely notes that "People don't buy what you do; they buy why you do it. And what you do simply proves what you believe."

When you write your Dear Author letter, the vision you create of your future will be deeply steeped in *why* you went to all the trouble of writing the book in the first place. What you hoped to accomplish will be at the forefront of your mind. And envisioning it as having come to pass will help to solidify that intention as you enter into the challenging stage of marketing and selling your book.

The byproduct of that is that you'll have a clear vision of what you want to accomplish. This makes it much easier to develop a marketing plan that skips all the little tangents and distractions that present themselves in the guise of "opportunities."

You'll have a yardstick you can measure your options against to determine whether they bring you closer to your goal. As a result, it will be easy to decide which to embrace and which to graciously decline for now.

If you find you want more help with this exercise, we are happy to guide you through the process and provide feedback on your Dear Author letter. Simply book a time with us at elbks.com/author-ex.

So, how do you do the Dear Author exercise? It's simple.

Imagine it's 18 months from now. Your future self has already put in the hard work needed to make your book a success. It hasn't been easy, but now you can look back on the journey and feel a deep sense of satisfaction in all that you've accomplished: for yourself, for your ideal reader and for your business.

It's certainly been a crazy journey! There were false starts along the way. Times when you thought about giving up or wondered if this was ever really going to happen. You realize there were things you wish you'd known when you first got started, but more importantly, there are things you never imagined the success of your book would achieve. And these are actually some of the things that bring the most satisfaction and joy to your life right now. It's hard to think that if you'd given up or hadn't worked so hard, you would have never experienced these things.

Suddenly, you're inspired! You decide to write a letter to your earlier self, the "you" that you are now, to share what the book has accomplished since its publication. It's somewhat of a walk down Memory Lane for you, but it helps you appreciate even more all that's been accomplished in the 18 short months since your book was published.

In the letter, you want to provide answers to the following questions:

1. Who was this book written for?

2. What were your hopes when the book was published?

3. How was your book received by readers?

4. What impact did the book's success have on your personal life and business?

5. How have you used those results to make the world a better place?

As with the Dear Reader letter, write this letter as if you're speaking directly to yourself, using first and second person ("I" and "you"). Fill it with encouragement and paint a clear picture of everything that has happened since the book came out.

The completed letter can be as long as you'd like. However, to keep from overwhelming yourself in the next step of the exercise, we recommend that it shouldn't be more than 2–3 pages long. Even at that length, it will help you look beyond the book's publication to the reason why you're writing it and what you hope to achieve as a result.

Many authors may find this exercise to be more challenging than the Dear Reader letter, because this one invites your future self to have a conversation with you now. Listen to that small inner voice. What is it telling you? What do you secretly hope and long for that this book could potentially accomplish? What pitfalls do you fear along the way?

This letter should be focused primarily on the positive. It is a triumphant letter that encourages you to press onward.

That doesn't mean you should ignore any niggling feelings that arise. By shedding light on them, you can proactively address them in the planning you do next. Consider it a chance to mitigate the risk of those things happening.

But most of all, let this letter be a voice of encouragement for you. Writing a book is hard. Marketing it is even harder. But being in touch with your "why" will help you press on when you're not having quite so much fun anymore.

This exercise is very much about getting in touch with your dearest hopes and dreams. So be real. Don't write the "acceptable" answers. Write what you really feel, without any filters. Nothing is too big or too unattainable. And don't generalize. Be specific! For example, don't just write that your book became a NYT bestseller. Specify how many copies were sold to achieve that.

Remember, this is not a questionnaire but an opportunity to dream about what you believe this book can accomplish. It's this dream that will enable you to lay a foundation for success, because it gives you something to chart your course by. As you write about the outcome, remember to be specific. When you can clearly identify what you hope to achieve, you can then plan how to make it happen. After all, you can't plan a route without knowing your destination, right?

When your letter is written, it should be something that makes you smile when you re-read it. If you can tap into the sense of satisfaction and gratitude your future self feels when they reflect on the past 18 months, then the exercise has been a success.

But wait! This exercise isn't over yet. Here's where the real value of the Dear Author letter comes in. It's not just a time-traveling joy ride. It's the key to mapping out your future plans and actions.

Once your letter is written, take a highlighter and mark all the accomplishments your future self has written you about. In a separate document, make a list of those accomplishments.

Then, shuffle the list items so they are presented in order of their *priority*, not achievability. The outcomes that have the most meaning to you or that would benefit your business the most should be at the top of the list. It doesn't matter how achievable they seem. The most significant ones go to the top of the list.

If you focus on too many goals at once, you won't truly make progress toward any of them. So, we're going to narrow the list to focus on just the first three. Then we recommend you print them out and post them where you can see them often.

It is important that all three of these goals be clearly communicated to everyone on your team, if you have one. Your book publicist, your launch team, your virtual assistant or social media manager, all need to know—these are your primary objectives right now. Any opportunity, conversation, connection or introduction that helps move you nearer any of those three goals is welcome. Everything else will need to be declined or deferred to a later time.

That's not to say the other outcomes you listed in your letter are irrelevant. But while you're pursuing your top three outcomes, you will not be dedicating any time to pursuing these additional goals. As your top goals are achieved, you can start adding the others, one at a time. But you should never have more than three you're specifically going after at one time.

With your top three goals in mind, you can begin putting a plan in place by objectively assessing where you are now and what it would take to achieve each of those goals. Map out the actions you need to take in order to implement your plan. Identify where you need mentors, coaches and partners to help you along the way, and what tools, training or additional resources you'll want.

Thanks to this exercise, you'll have a clear vision of what you want to accomplish, you'll be able to map out a plan to take you from where you currently are to where you want to be, and you'll be invigorated by the sense of satisfaction imparted by your future self.

That's why we recommend that, when your own Dear Author letter is complete, you refer to it regularly. The only way it can serve as encouragement to you during challenging times and a beacon to you for direction is if you remember it's there and re-read it often.

CASE STUDY: SUSANNA LILLER

One of our authors, Susanna Liller (susannaliller.com), is a huge fan of vision boards, so she had no difficulty grasping the simplicity and power of the Dear Author letter. We looked forward to seeing her letter and discovering what she saw as the ideal outcomes for her book's future.

Typically, with most authors we've shared this exercise with, I've had to challenge them to stretch themselves more. The goals they came up with were easily attainable and well within their comfort zones. But there's little growth to be found in a comfort zone. So we asked these authors to challenge themselves more and truly think about what they wanted most.

We didn't have to do that with Susanna, though. She nailed her letter in one take, and put us to shame a little in the process.

Her book is *You Are a Heroine: A Retelling of the Hero's Journey* (elbks.com/heroine) and it explores how Joseph Campbell's "hero's journey" plays out differently when a woman is the central figure of the story. For example, while men may slay their dragons, women tend to view them as protectors, so their more natural response is to ignore or embrace them, depending on their current mindset.

Here's the letter her future self wrote.

> September 13, 2020, Friday
>
> Dear Susanna,
>
> I'm picturing you sitting at your desk in your office those many months ago—18!! They went by so quickly. And now look at you. So many changes. So many good and amazing changes. What if you hadn't tried? What if you had listened to those Threshold Guardians in your head? But you persevered. Five years of writing. Your time with Jack, then Katy, then kdb, then telling kdb you didn't want her to do your website, then Tara and Mark and Annie—and the others who have come to you with their valuable help. It's just like that Campbell quotation you love so much and that's the epigraph of chapter 8: if you follow your bliss you find yourself on a road that's been waiting for you all along with people who have the same kind of bliss and they open doors for you. So many doors were opened for you, Susanna.

But you had to walk through those doors—and you did! Hey, those words are from your song that became so popular (can you believe that??): "Walk through that door, don't stop to look behind..." I love that song, Susanna.

You believed in your book and you kept moving forward. And you got the help you needed. Listening to Patty, "You need to give your book over to an expert," and reaching out to Emerald Lake Books. That was Divine Guidance to be sure. And you enlisted the help of Annie at the recommendation of Tara. That's what really got the ball rolling for you. You have made one good decision after another, Susanna, and I am so proud of you!

I know that your intent was to collect all the content of what you shared with women over the twelve years of Ruby Slippers workshops and retreats in one place so it could be disseminated to a wider group of women. You wanted to "get it down," to document what you taught and facilitated in those gatherings because you truly believed/believe it would help women—and it has. I know you wanted to encourage women's confidence and courage to do what they felt called to do by sharing the heroine's journey model. You wanted them to know that they already were heroines based on what they had already done. You wanted them to gain the confidence that comes from identifying with the heroine persona and the heroine's journey. They were already traveling that path. And they got that, Susanna! Your message got out there and they bought and read the book—in droves.

Oh, and how wonderful that Lisa, Maureen and Pamela came out with you to speak about the book and their journeys in all those different venues—across the country. How much fun it was for the four of you to do it together—and look how much it built success for each of them!

Of course, it helped immensely that *You Are a Heroine* came out at the beginning of a new and energized empowerment movement for women, Susanna. The Women's March, the Me-Too Movement, the influx of women into our government... all of that was building as you put your book out into the world. I know you didn't plan it, but if you had—you couldn't have planned the timing any better!! Women loved your message that they were heroines! I know you kept running out of t-shirts because they especially loved the "Be Your Own Heroine" and "Embrace Your Dragon" ones. It became a "thing" and a unifying thing, which I know was also important to you—women coming together.

(Oh, and... I know you're especially pleased to see the women's circles, facilitated by the women you trained, cropping up more and more. They are doing the personal strategic planning exercise together...

the circle exercise... the comfort zone challenge. That recent facilitator training you gave in Del Mar with Jeanne was so much fun.)

You wanted women to see that at our very core, we are the same, traveling the same life path—though we are also unique. There was such divisiveness eighteen months ago and you wanted the book to point out how we're the same, united by this heroine framework, so that women could work together to change the world. Just like Campbell in *The Hero With a Thousand Faces* was pointing out that the same "hero's journey myth" was in all cultures throughout time—emphasizing that as people we, too, are the same, telling the same monomyth, as he called it, to teach the same values to our cultures.

And I know your hope was also to build the feminine energy in our world. I know you strongly believe that the world will benefit from more feminine energy. What's that Obama quote from his Barnard 2012 Commencement speech? "Women shape not only their own destiny but the destiny of this nation and of this world." Women got that message too as more and more read your book, focused on hearing their calls and poured themselves into improving our world.

It didn't hurt, did it, that Oprah heard of the book and featured you on SuperSoul Sunday!! That was quite the event, wasn't it? And there were other similar events just as amazing, weren't there? Phew! It's been a whirlwind, but a good whirlwind! All helping to get your message out—we are heroines! We matter! And we are called to develop ourselves authentically, not according to someone else's expectations, but unique to who we are—which is exactly what happens on the heroine's journey. And the more we shine our own light in this world, the better our world becomes.

(And who could have predicted the impact of your dragonheart logo? Mark must have been channeling some special spiritual guidance when he created it. Women so connected to that! Befriend and love your dragon, your "dark places" and bring the light in—unleash your power! Of course, it was perfect that 2019 was the year that Game of Thrones came back for another season and that show has such a great heroine who has some pretty powerful dragons. Good timing yet again!)

Everything you wanted the book to do has happened, Susanna! It has been a wonderful journey since the launch. I know you thought initially that it would be overwhelming, but because of those "helping hands" coming at just the right time, it has been such an empowering and joyful journey for you—and your family, too. (I know it was hard to let go of Liller Consulting, because you loved that work and you helped people in that capacity, too. I think you knew that was inevitable, though, as your success grew with the book.) The book has sold so many copies and you have had so many recognitions: the awards, the invitations to speak, the huge media coverage. It just kept building but it didn't get overwhelming. It just kept getting better and better. And the financial boon was unexpected (but remember, the heroine receives a boon at the end of her journey). We passed a million copies in six months! Weren't Tara and Mark pleased!! I remember yours and Robin's discussion about 500 copies in five years. Haha! I guess you were off a bit—it was the best thing to gift him with that boat he's always wanted. And now, here you are, too, in the lake cottage you've always wanted.

Bottom line, there are girls and women out there who now know they are heroines on an empowering path and they are connected to each other in a way they never knew before. They believe in themselves in a way that wasn't possible before. They don't point to someone else and say, "She's a heroine." They point to themselves and have the courage to follow through on what their own inner voice is urging them to do. We are all doing it together and, Susanna, you had the courage, you heroine you, to let your voice be heard! Kudos to you!!

I'd better end here and let you get back to writing. I know the lake is the best place to write. People are waiting for this next book, Susanna. They want to hear more about the spiritual aspect of the journey because that's what super powers the journey, as you well know. Keep writing, speaking and sharing with us, and God bless you.

Much love,
Your Future Self

P.S. You know how I believe in signs. Remember that I said to you when Dorothy's ruby slippers were found in September of 2018 that that was a good sign for you? It was, wasn't it!? Keep clicking your ruby slippers, Susanna!

You don't have to understand every point in Susanna's letter to herself to see how much freedom she gave herself to dream, and dream big! And that's why I said it put us to shame a little. Even as her publisher, reading this letter, I almost choked when I read that we'd sold a million copies in six months. Of course, we'd love that to happen for her, but it was definitely a stretch goal for an unknown author. However, knowing *what* she wanted to accomplish enabled her to devise plans to help her attain that goal, and having a plan meant her chances of accomplishing what she wanted were that much higher.

Yardstick for Marketing Plan

A well-executed Dear Author letter reveals multiple goals you'd like to achieve. So, the next step is to go through the letter, identify those goals, prioritize them, and then start outlining the steps necessary to get from where you are now to where you'd like to be 18 months from now.

If we go through Susanna's Dear Author letter, we find these are the results she wanted most to achieve:

1. Her song became popular.

2. The book's message got out there and the book itself was being read in droves.

3. She had speaking events across the country with Lisa, Maureen and Pamela, people featured in her book.

4. She ran out of her "#BeAHeroine" and "Embrace Your Dragons" branded t-shirt merchandise.

5. There were trained facilitators leading women's circles.

6. She led facilitator training in Del Mar with her friend Jeanne.

7. Women united because of this heroine framework.

8. The feminine energy in our world was increased.

9. The book was featured on Oprah's SuperSoul Sunday.

10. The dragonheart logo resonated with people and had a significant impact.

11. Susanna successfully transitioned from her primary business, Liller Consulting, and was working in her side business full-time.

12. The book received numerous recognitions, including awards, speaking invitations and media coverage.

13. We sold 1 million copies of the book in its first six months.

14. She bought her husband, Robin, a boat.

15. She bought the lake cottage.

16. Women began to understand they are heroines, connected to each other, and believing in themselves.

17. She had begun writing Book #2, detailing the spiritual aspect of the journey.

After some discussion and soul-searching, she decided that her Top 3 goals were as follows:

✓ To sell 1 million copies in 6 months.

✓ For her message to get out there in a big way, with her book being read in droves.

✓ For women to know they are heroines (an on-going thing) by connecting to each other more and believing in themselves (via self-led workshops).

Initially, she felt that items 5 and 6 were something she would pursue later. However, as we discussed potential plans and the steps necessary to accomplish her top 3 goals, it became clear that there needed to be more people promoting the concepts from her book than just herself. There were a few reasons for this decision.

First, as she sat with the idea of teaching the retreats and workshops herself, she felt drained. She was sapped of all energy and knew that facilitating workshops herself was not how she wanted to spend her time. Instead, she felt energized by the idea of doing more intimate retreats with smaller groups of women, to really help them each make progress on their own, unique Heroine's Journey.

Yet to get her message "out there in a big way," she needed the power of leverage. She needed more than just herself sharing the concepts from her book. And these concepts needed to be shared with larger groups, which meant less intimate settings.

As a result, we decided that the steps she needed to take to accomplish her Top 3 goals were going to require the following:

✓ Conducting the workshop a few times herself, so she could test and tweak the content.

✓ Capturing testimonials from workshop attendees to use in subsequent marketing materials.

✓ Documenting how to run the workshop in a consistent and easily repeatable manner.

✓ Finding existing coaches who would be interested in learning her methodology.

✓ Defining a certification process for facilitators, as well as a licensing agreement for using her material.

✓ Conducting certification training for qualified, interested coaches.

✓ Creating VIP retreats that past workshop participants could attend with her to dive deeper into what they've learned.

This particular plan would then enable certified facilitators to lay the groundwork with larger groups, while she guided people along a more in-depth course.

The steps we outlined would all serve to help her sell a significant number of copies of her book, get her message out there so her book was being read in droves, and help women to grasp the concepts of the book.

But it also respected the fact that there were aspects of the journey she was passionate about participating in herself and others she was quite content to allow other people to share in.

Had she not done the Dear Author exercise, the plan she would have developed might not have been as focused or clear to her, and more trial and error would have been involved in figuring out how to grow her business with her book.

This is what you can anticipate the Dear Author letter doing for you as well. It allows you to imagine a future for yourself, see what feels "right" and "good" to you, and then create an action plan that gets you from the here-and-now to the future you want with as few detours and distractions as possible.

But don't just take my word for it. Here's what Susanna had to say five months later, when we asked her whether she found the exercise helpful:

> What benefit did I get from the Dear Author letter? It opened me up to a vision of what's truly possible. As a writer, I am well acquainted with the limits we put on ourselves as soon as we begin a sentence. That inner critic always hovers in the background, telling me I don't have what it takes. That's the "Threshold Guardian" in Heroine's Journey-speak.
>
> Living a successful life is about learning how to circumvent or quiet that limiting voice. If you can do this, then you can follow the limitless inner guidance that comes from an entirely different place, your soul, your heart—however you label that wise part of yourself.

The Dear Author letter exercise helps you do just that. Writing the letter from eighteen months in the future helps you silence the critic and dream, unhindered. That's when you get a glimpse of what's really possible for yourself and it's stunning! You can then live into *that* vision of your future instead of defaulting into the stunted one. Every time I read my letter I feel an inner leap of joy! It resonates. Yes, this is my heroine's journey!

When you find yourself wondering what you've gotten yourself into, your Dear Author letter will serve as a reminder as to why you began the journey in the first place. So, be proud of it. Read it often. It will help guide you along the course you've charted for yourself and your book.

Do the Work!

THE CLARITY THAT'S PROVIDED by the Dear Author exercise helps you identify the primary things you want to achieve with your book. And the Dear Reader exercise helps you understand the needs of your reader.

The next step, then, is to ensure that you've laid a foundation that supports your reader's success, as well as that of your business.

Map out the steps the reader needs to go through to experience the transformation they want for themselves. Then ask yourself, what do I need to create to facilitate that journey?

Perhaps it's a supportive community. In which case, you may want to explore the idea of creating a membership site or a Facebook group.

Or perhaps it's more detailed interactive content. In which case, you may want to create a video course, group coaching program, or quiz-based online self-assessment that provides tailored information specific to the reader's wants and needs.

The idea here is to consider what resources you can (and want) to offer that will help your reader along the way and then make sure you've created those offerings before the book is launched.

It's important that these be ready as soon as the book is released, because if you do have a sudden burst of interest from readers, you don't want to have to tell them they need to wait for whatever it was you were going to offer them.

Once you've addressed the reader's needs, go back and look at the top three priorities you identified as a result of the Dear Author exercise. Then, map out a plan for how to get from where you are now to where you want to be in 18 months. What do you need in order to accomplish that? Are there connections you want to make? Training you need? Products to create? Have you anticipated your reader's needs, and do you have other products or services they will want or need?

Simply identifying what is still needed isn't enough, though. Now it's time to do the hard work.

If, like Susanna, you want to sell a million copies of your book in six months, you have to figure out how you're going to leverage other people's audiences. That means building relationships with influencers and organizations who serve your ideal reader *before* you're in need of their help.

It also means building a community for your readers where they can share, learn and grow. Susanna went so far as to have branded merchandise created, including t-shirts, totes and mugs. Since part of Susanna's goal in writing was to help women embrace their "heroineism," this enabled her Heroines to celebrate their heroineism in a way that readily identifies them as part of the growing Heroine community.

Each author's map for how to get from where they are to where they want to go is going to be different. But now is the time to figure it all out, incorporate it into your book, and prepare to meet your reader's needs.

When you continually approach your book from the standpoint of "what's in it for them," instead of "what's in it for me," the value will speak for itself and people will want more from you, because generosity and authenticity resonates.

In his book *Secrets of Closing the Sale*, Zig Ziglar wrote, "You can have everything in life you want, if you will just help enough other people get what they want." Your book is your opportunity to help other people get what they want. Focus on that and the rest will come, so make sure you're prepared for it!

EMBRACING THE PURPOSE
BEYOND THE PURPOSE

THE FIRST TWO GOALS WE WORKED ON relate to the outcomes you want for your reader and your business. The third goal in the Publish with Purpose framework is more altruistic. This goal is about the purpose *beyond* the purpose of your book. This is where your personal passion gets to benefit from the work you've done.

Here's an excerpt from my own Dear Author letter for this book, which shares what's meant by "the purpose beyond the purpose."

> By writing *Publish with Purpose*, you inspired so many positive people to share their unique messages. That in itself uplifted their readers. But by helping those same authors see ways to increase the monetary potential of their books, you gave them the key to creating their own financial freedom, along with a strong desire to give back in whatever ways had meaning to them.
>
> The resulting increase in donations to charities and nonprofits, the marked increase in volunteerism across the country, and the hope for a better life and

a better world that you've sparked in so many people through this book has transcended the niche it was written for and inspired people in other industries to re-evaluate how they do business, so that they too can make a bigger impact in the world. It has blurred political, racial and religious lines, and reduced polarization among the populace. Instead of people focusing on what's in it for them, they recognize that if they focus on helping others first, the rest will fall into place. And that's been a beautiful and unanticipated outcome of publishing this book.

My hope is that when we, as authors, as human beings, put our minds to providing value to others and helping them improve their own situations, the effort will have a ripple effect.

One of my favorite authors, Andy Andrews, shares a story in his book *The Butterfly Effect: How Your Life Matters* (elbks.com/butterflyeffect). Andrews tells how, in a doctoral thesis written in 1963, Edward Lorenz theorized that a butterfly might flap its wings, moving molecules of air into motion that in turn moved other molecules of air, eventually becoming able to shift weather patterns on the other side of the world.

Of course, all the authorities at that time agreed that the theory was ridiculous. It wasn't until the mid-'90s that physicists authenticated the Lorenz hypothesis. Commonly called "The Butterfly Effect," it has now been granted the status of a law.

When we are willing to take the time to help others, lend our influence to a favorite cause, and find ways to "give back" that are meaningful to us and to the message we're passionate about sharing, we are, in effect, butterflies whose wings will have far-reaching impacts.

The best way to illustrate this point is with another case study.

CASE STUDY: MARC YOUNGQUIST

Let me tell you a bit about another one of our authors, Marc Youngquist (marcyoungquist.com).

Master Sergeant Marc Youngquist served in the military and law enforcement for over 40 years. In 2003–2004, his unit, the 143rd Military Police Company of the Connecticut Army National Guard, was deployed to Iraq with orders to recruit, train and prepare an Iraqi police force.

The conditions his unit experienced were horrible. They endured everything from training for desert conditions in the dead of winter without the appropriate gear to driving through the night trying to find Baghdad with pieces of a map puzzle. Their mission took them into war zones without an adequate supply of soldiers, weapons or ammo.

Despite seeing combat almost every day for a year in Iraq, very few articles were ever written back home about the unit. And when they returned to Connecticut, Marc sometimes found himself having surprising conversations with mutual acquaintances of his fellow soldiers—not one of them knew any of the details of what their friends, coworkers, employees and relatives had done in Iraq.

One day, Marc was giving a presentation for Veteran's Day at a local middle school. He shared a story that demonstrated the dedication and bravery displayed by the soldiers from the 143rd on one particular, hellish day during their deployment.

Three soldiers assigned to the active-duty unit the 143rd was working with were attacked and suffered life-threatening injuries. Six soldiers from the 143rd went to their aid. Under fire, the three injured soldiers were carried across an open area to safety. Unfortunately, one of them, Specialist Rachel Bosveld, died as a result of the wounds she received.

After the presentation, a teacher approached Marc. She asked if he knew a close friend of hers, Andrea, who was stationed in Iraq. It turned out that Andrea was one of the six soldiers who had performed the rescue and gone on to receive a medal of valor. The teacher had never heard this story about her friend or that she'd received recognition for her bravery.

It turned out that Andrea's boss, then-Governor Dannel P. Malloy, had never heard about it either, even though she was assigned to his personal security detail.

So, Marc set out to tell the story of the unsung heroes in his unit and to ensure that state and military leaders connected their supply and budgetary decisions to the resulting outcomes.

That was his main purpose in writing *The 143rd in Iraq* (elbks. com/143rd).

However, the purpose *beyond* the purpose was something different. In Marc's case, he wasn't looking to build a business. He didn't necessarily want recognition for himself as an author as much as he wanted recognition for his unit and all they had done in spite of an abhorrent lack of support.

By writing the book, he generated that recognition. By selling the book, he used the proceeds to contribute to military-themed nonprofits that are doing work he believes in.

His purpose *beyond* the purpose was to provide support and encouragement to his brothers-in-arms and their families. And book sales simply became a means to an end.

But his book also opened opportunities to speak in schools, helping young people understand intangible concepts like bravery and sacrifice. And the ripple effect of his actions will be felt through the lives he's impacted as a result of sharing his story.

Identifying Your Purpose Beyond the Purpose

The Dear Reader and Dear Author exercises provide clarity about the purpose of your book and what you're trying to accomplish with it, both for the reader and for yourself.

However, this particular goal is often more altruistic. It's about making a difference in the world, in whatever way resonates most with you, with what you have to share and with what you've gained as a result.

We are all on this journey together. You don't have to have accomplished a certain level of success to be able to make a difference. You don't even have to have written a book. But no matter where you are on your life's journey, there are people who have helped you get there and people who want to get to where you are now. In honor of those who have helped or inspired you, remember to do the same for others.

When you can tie your book into this, it elevates it in your heart and gives it a whole new purpose and meaning.

For some authors, that may mean reading at Story Hour somewhere, volunteering for literacy programs for incarcerated youth, or mentoring someone who's coming up through the ranks. For others, it might mean supporting your favorite nonprofit, organizing a book fair, reading to shut-ins or hospital patients, or donating your books to those who can't afford it.

Another of our authors, Linda Lattimore, wrote a book called *Solutionaries* (elbks.com/solutionaries) that's aimed at a Baby Boomer audience. Despite that, she tailored her content into a leadership presentation she can give at a girls' school in her area. Teenagers aren't her business's demographic, but she knows that if these young women learn the principles she shares earlier in life, they'll benefit from it. So, it's her way to make a difference in her local community.

Just prior to publishing this book, I shared this chapter with my writers' critique group. I know that this last part of our framework is more nebulous than the others, and I was concerned whether I'd explained it well enough to convey its importance. My friend, Andrea O'Connor, surprised me with her feedback.

> This resonated deeply for me. I wouldn't change a word. It set me to thinking about my goal for my book, *Woodson Falls*, which was to both intrigue and entertain the reader. My goal for myself was to enjoy the simple joy of writing. But, as I read this, I struggled with just what my purpose beyond the purpose might be—and I found it! It is the opportunity to share the *process* of writing that publishing this book would provide. Writing is something that means so much to me that I'd like to help others enjoy it too. Thank you!

The excitement that Andrea felt as she shared this with me is exactly what I hope you find too.

There is no right or wrong answer to this part of the equation. It's simply about exploring the opportunities to give back in some way that your book will create for you, separate from what the reader experiences and your business benefits from.

This is often the outcome that shines brighter than all the rest for you, simply because of the joy it brings you. It's not about money, influence or fame. It's about personal satisfaction.

And that's what finding the purpose beyond the purpose of your book is all about. It's about finding ways to use your book, its content or the visibility that success brings to give back in ways that are meaningful to you and those whose lives you touch.

WHERE TO FROM HERE?

IF YOU'VE TAKEN THE TIME to do the exercises as you've read through this book, you now have a clearly defined set of goals you want to accomplish.

✓ You have aligned your ideal customer and reader.

✓ You know what they want and expect.

✓ You have identified the best ways to bring value to them.

✓ You have permitted yourself to dream about what the success of your book would mean to you, your business and your family.

✓ And you have considered the potential impact your book could have on making the world a better place in a way that's significant to you.

More importantly, you have assessed where you are now and where you want to go, as well as what's needed to accomplish your goals.

The whole point of the Publish with Purpose framework is to be continually aware of the outcomes you want to achieve. For it is only in this way that you can chart a course to reach your chosen destination.

We wish you well on your journey, and may you achieve the success you desire, as you help others find their own success!

Thank you for reading *Publish with Purpose*. If you've enjoyed reading this book, please leave a review on your favorite review site. It helps me reach more readers who may benefit from the information.

Emerald Lake Books has developed a workbook to use in conjunction with workshops we offer based on *Publish With Purpose*. If you'd like your own copy of the workbook, you can download it at emeraldlakebooks.com/pwpbonus. And thanks for joining us on this journey toward purposeful publishing!

ABOUT THE AUTHOR

TARA ALEMANY DEFIES A SIMPLE DEFINITION. She is a multi-award winning author, speaker, business consultant and publisher, as well as a serial entrepreneur.

Although she's started many businesses during her career, her favorite by far is Emerald Lake Books, which she co-owns with her best friend, Mark Gerber. This hybrid publishing company specializes in working with positive people who have an engaging, exciting or entertaining message to share with the world.

Using a unique, goal-oriented approach to publishing, Tara combines her business and publishing knowledge to help her authors set and attain goals for their readers, their brands and their books.

And many of those books have gone on to win international awards and recognition, thanks to Emerald Lake's "Publish with Purpose" framework.

Tara's latest book, *Publish with Purpose*, reveals the unique process developed by Emerald Lake Books to help their authors set and attain their own goals.

In addition to publishing, consulting, writing and speaking, Tara serves on the Board of Directors for a Christian writers' critique group, acting as both president and chaplain of the group. In her spare time, she is a winemaker, a military Mom to 2 young people (one of each), step-Mom to 1 lovable mutt, and is owned by a black cat.

If you're interested in having Tara come speak to your group or organization, you can contact her at elbks.com/alemany.

And if you'd like to explore the possibility of working with Emerald Lake Books to have us publish your book and coach you through the Publish with Purpose framework, we invite you to complete an application at elbks.com/application.

Acknowledgments

WRITING ACKNOWLEDGMENTS IS OFTEN the most challenging part of completing a book. There is always the fear of forgetting to mention someone significant, and of not finding just the right words to express the gratitude one feels so keenly.

But let me start off my acknowledgements a little more generally, then narrow it down to the more specific.

As always, I am so very grateful for the love, support and encouragement of my family. My mom and dad, Chris Freeman and Nick Alemany, my sister and brother-in-law, Rachel and Brian Dickinson, my children, Eliza and Timothy Alemany. They don't always "get" why I do what I do, but they love me all the same. And when my 19-year-old son comes home from a long day of work and still listens to me prattle on about the accomplishments of the day, that's a pretty darn special thing!

Many in my church family are dear to me as well, but I want to especially acknowledge Jill Finch and Clayton Winters, who have gone out of their way over the twenty-one years that I've known them to support me in all that I do, and to make me feel like a part of their family. Jill is one of the most loving, generous and supportive people I know, never letting the hardships of life hold her back. It seems like there isn't a thing this adventurous woman isn't up for! And it's always fun to hear about her latest exploits, whether it's with the car club, ski patrol or traveling.

Clay is the cofounder of Boyds Mills Press, the trade book division of Highlights for Children. He has served in almost every job imaginable connected with trade publishing, selling and marketing books as a retailer, wholesaler and representative of trade publishing houses both giant and modest. So when I first launched Emerald Lake Books, I asked if I could take him to breakfast and pick his brains for a bit. I'll never forget sitting at our local restaurant, sharing my (then limited) vision for Emerald Lake Books and having him pause and then ask me, "Why in the world would you want to go into publishing?" I didn't have a good enough answer for you then, Papa Clay. But hopefully, this book sheds a little more light on my wacky notion.

Of course, *Publish with Purpose* would not have been possible without the authors who have entrusted their manuscripts to Emerald Lake Books. Many of your stories have made it into this book as case studies because of how compelling they are. When I first started publishing your books, I didn't have a goal-oriented framework to work within. It wasn't even on my mind at the time. It was only through helping each of you that I began to see the importance of truly understanding what you wanted to accomplish with your book, what your goals were. Many of you served as willing "guinea pigs" as we tested these techniques, and adapted and expanded them to make them our own. And many of you encouraged us to continue what we were doing because it was making a difference for you. So, thank you for being part of the Emerald Lake Books family. I truly appreciate each and every one of you.

I need to acknowledge Justin Spizman as well. I first heard him talk about his Dear Reader exercise at a conference in October 2017. By mid-November, it had taken root in my imagination, and I began sketching out a framework we might be able to use to help our authors accomplish exactly what they wanted most with their books. In the next few months, the exercise grew and developed into the expanded version we went on to use with our authors, and then I created the subsequent Dear Author exercise as a companion to it. The combination of these two activities is a powerful tool for any author, and our versions of them may never have existed if you hadn't shared your Dear Reader exercise with us to begin with. So thank you!

Lastly, there's Mark Gerber, the yin to my yang. And this is where I fear my words will fail me most. But you already know what I want to say. Right? Nothing I accomplish would feel right without you. Everything we've built these past few years... None of it would have been possible without talking it all through with you and figuring out how to make things our own. Emerald Lake Books would not be what it is today without you in it, and I know that my own life would be all the poorer for that. So thank you for finally caving in and agreeing to work with me. I love what we're creating together and look forward to what the years ahead hold in store for us.

For more great books, please visit us at
emeraldlakebooks.com.

EMERALD LAKE
BOOKS

Made in the USA
Las Vegas, NV
11 August 2024

93662477R00074